HELPING

THE CHILD

WHO DOESN'T FIT IN

DATE DUE

			PRINTED IN U.S.A.

HELPING
THE CHILD
WHO DOESN'T FIT IN

Clinical Psychologists
Stephen Nowicki, Jr. and Marshall P. Duke
Decipher the Hidden Dimensions
of Social Rejection

With a Foreword by Bonnie R. Strickland

PEACHTREE
PUBLISHERS

Also by the authors

Teaching Your Child the Language of Social Success

Published by
PEACHTREE PUBLISHERS, LTD.
1700 Chattahoochee Avenue
Atlanta, Georgia 30318-2112

Book design by Kathryn D. Mothershed
Cover illustration by Laura L. Seeley

20 19 18 17 16 15

Manufactured in the United States of America

Library of Congress Cataloging–in–Publication Data

Nowicki, Stephen.
        Helping the child who doesn't fit in /
Stephen Nowicki, Jr., Marshall P. Duke.
              p.   cm.
        Includes bibliographic references and appendix.
        ISBN 1-56145-025-1
        1. Nonverbal communication in children. 2. Non-
verbal communication (Psychology) 3. Interpersonal relationships in children. 4. Interpersonal relations. I. Duke, Marshall
P. II. Title.
  BF723.C57N67   1991   91-18373
  155.4'1369—dc20   CIP

To our parents, who taught us so much about belonging

CONTENTS

◇

FOREWORD

◇

Children are our greatest treasure. We welcome infants with high hopes for their health and happiness. Typically, our first question is whether the infant is physically healthy and intellectually alert. From then on, we try to expose our children to experiences that will enhance their physical and cognitive development, delighting in their first words and the energy they bring to their new world.

Parents, educators, and psychologists do all that is within their knowledge and power to arrange opportunities for the growing child to become intellectually curious and competent. We recognize that cognitive skills, such as language, learning, and memory are necessary for a child to navigate and master an expanding environment. Intelligence tests abound, and we watch carefully for any indications that a child may be having difficulty learning to speak, read, or write. Indeed, we have become quite skilled in assessing learning disabilities.

While we emphasize the intellectual and cognitive skills, we know much less about other, perhaps equally important aspects of a child's development. Few, if any, instruments are available to indicate the degree to which a child is emotionally and/or socially skilled. In fact, until the pioneering work of Nowicki and Duke, along with a few other researchers in this area, little attention has been given to clarifying ways in which nonverbal behavior can affect a child's social acceptance and competence.

Nonverbal communication is a powerful index of feelings and experiences and an ever-present reality for all of us and our children. The understanding and exchange of nonverbal information constitutes a "language" of its own, a language that is described simply and eloquently by Nowicki and Duke. They propose ways in which children may be deficient in the receiving and sending of nonverbal messages. For example, some children may not be able to recognize particular emotional signals or be able to express their own feelings to others. Thus, deficits in this other language may explain why some children are developmentally delayed in their social and emotional interactions even though they are of normal intelligence, or perhaps even intellectually gifted.

This book, and the research that supports its findings, represents that rare blending of important new scientific insights with practical applications. It brings us new ways of helping children learn a new language, rich in emotional meaning, and necessary for healthy interpersonal relationships.

—Bonnie R. Strickland, Ph.D., ABPP
Past President of the American Psychological Association
Professor of Psychology, University of Massachusetts at Amherst

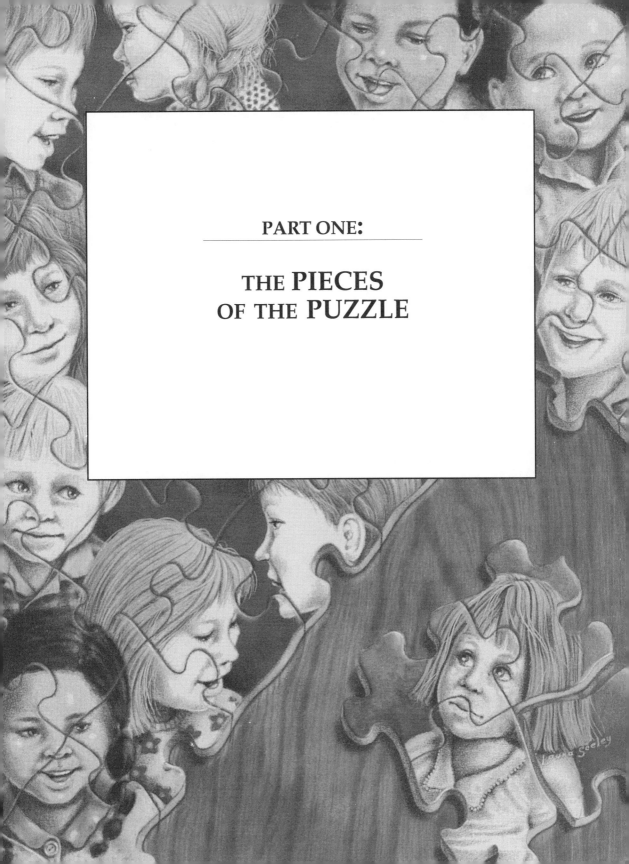

PART ONE:

THE PIECES
OF THE PUZZLE

INTRODUCTION:

THE PUZZLE
OF SOCIAL REJECTION

THE PUZZLE OF SOCIAL REJECTION

◇

We all know children who just can't seem to get life "right." They really want others to like them, but the harder they try, the worse they seem to do. They are like pieces of a puzzle that do not fit in. They are the "square pegs," the fifth wheels, the ones who are picked last for teams, the children who sit alone in a corner of the playground, wondering why others don't like them. Sometimes they're called hurtful names such as "nerd," "geek," and "weirdo." At other times, they're treated as if they don't exist.

These children desperately want to fit in and have friends, but they usually fail to do so. They have been largely ignored or rejected, not only by their peers but also by well-meaning adults, who have not known the source of these children's troubles and have therefore not known how to help. Decades of research and clinical observation have led us to believe that we have found one such source, and we can tell you how to help. Specifically, *we believe that many children who don't fit in have trouble using nonverbal communication.* That is, they have difficulty communicating non-verbal information through facial expressions, postures, gestures, interpersonal distance, tone of voice, clothing, and the like.

These children frequently break the rules of nonverbal communication. They may stand too close to others, touch them inappropriately, or misunderstand and misinterpret friendly actions. These difficulties can lead to painful social rejection, especially when—and we believe this is a crucial part of the process—the child has little or no idea that he or she is the source of the problem. Rejection can lead to feelings of anxiety, sadness, loneliness, bewilderment, and worthlessness. What a terrible burden for a child to bear while growing up—and since relationships become more important and more complex as we move into adolescence, this burden can grow increasingly heavier and more harmful.

M any children who don't fit in have trouble using nonverbal communication. Nonverbal information is communicated through facial expressions, postures, gestures, interpersonal distance, tone of voice, clothing, and the like.

Do you remember the kids everybody liked when you were in school? They were the ones who did everything "right." They weren't always the most attractive or intelligent, but they were the people everybody wanted to be around. They were fun and easy to be with. We think that children such as these have the very set of interpersonal abilities and skills that the rejected children lack. It isn't just a question of manners; these likable children know how to communicate nonverbally with friends and adults. This ability gives them the foundation needed to make friends and to survive childhood successfully.

When we say "nonverbal communication," you may be thinking we mean "body language," and you may be wondering why some children are good at this and others aren't. Well, "body language" is really only a part of nonverbal communication. Indeed, many believe that nonverbal communication is a fully developed language that functions side by side with verbal language. The reason why some children don't learn this nonverbal language is that we don't teach it formally. While we go to school to learn the grammar of the spoken language, there is little formal training available for the learning of nonverbal language. It is primarily taught (on an unconscious basis) by parents and family members, and it is typically learned through observation. Since we only learn nonverbal language informally, in a hit-or-miss kind of way, some children miss out or fail to learn about one or more of the nonverbal rules. Thus, they may have a *nonverbal communication deficit.* If a young child has not learned how to use gestures or other nonverbal behavior to communicate, he or she may arrive at school unprepared to understand such behavior from others.

We hope to show you how to detect whether your child is suffering from a nonverbal communication deficit, and how to work with your child to correct the problem. Often all it takes is assessing the problem, explaining it to the child, and working through some corrective procedures. In other cases, assessment may reveal a more extensive problem which will require professional intervention. In either case, the first step to helping your child is to become aware of the importance of nonverbal language.

The Language of Relationships

Nonverbal language is usually seen by others as a reliable reflection of how we actually feel. A classic set of studies by Albert Mehrabian showed that in face-to-face interactions, 55 percent of the emotional meaning of a message is expressed through facial, postural, and gestural means, and 38 percent of the emotional meaning is transmitted through the tone of voice. *Only seven percent of the emotional meaning is actually expressed with words.* Most of us know this unconsciously, and on almost every occasion in which words and nonverbal language express different messages, we will believe the nonverbal message. Take for example a teacher who has just finished a math lesson and is about to dismiss her class for recess. At the same time that she says, "Please ask me as many questions about the math lesson as you want to," she looks

Nonverbal language is usually seen by others as a reliable reflection of how we actually feel. On almost every occasion in which words are pitted against nonverbal language, we will believe what is being transmitted nonverbally.

at her watch. The verbal message says, "I invite questions and I have plenty of time to answer them," but the nonverbal message says, "I am in a hurry and I really don't have time to answer any questions." Most students will pick up what the teacher is "saying" as she looks at her watch, but the type of child who innocently misreads or ignores that cue and asks a long, involved question is the focus of this book—a child who doesn't understand the meaning of nonverbal language.

Because nonverbal communication is normally seen as a reliable gauge of feelings, serious misunderstandings can occur if we fail to interpret nonverbal messages correctly, or if we send nonverbal messages that do not accurately reflect our emotions. This possibility is made even more potentially damaging by the fact that our nonverbal behaviors are often seen as reflecting our very emotional stability.

Consider the differences between two adolescent boys, David and Tom:

David, in talking with another boy, says, "We seen the car going down Main Street. It were going about fifty miles an hour. I couldn't do nothing to stop it. It were flustrating."

What conclusions would you draw about David from overhearing his conversation? We believe that one of your first judgments would involve his intelligence or educational level or perhaps both.

Now let's look at Tom. He decides to go to a movie, a light comedy. After paying for his ticket, he enters the theater and looks around. There are only five other people in a theater large enough for two hundred. Tom walks down the aisle and stops where one person is sitting in the middle of a row. He walks into that row until he reaches the seat next to the stranger and promptly sits down.

What would you conclude about Tom after observing his behavior? We believe that if you focus on his seat selection, you will conclude that Tom is behaving strangely. Think of yourself as being that one person sitting in the middle of the seventh row of a movie theater that can hold hundreds of people. What are your conclusions about Tom, and how does he make you feel? If you are like the participants in our workshops, you think that something is psychologically wrong with Tom, and he makes you anxious, uneasy, uncomfortable and afraid. Further, unlike David, Tom's nonverbal language is likely to spur you to action—to get up and leave.

◆

Our point here is that more often than not, mistakes in verbal communication will lead others to regard the child who makes the mistake as uneducated and/or unintelligent. On the other hand, mistakes in nonverbal communication will usually get a child labeled as weird or strange. When a person makes a mistake in verbal communication, we make judgments about his or her intellectual *abilities*. In contrast, when a person commits an error in nonverbal communication, we are more prone to make judgments about his or her mental *stability*. It is one thing to be around someone we consider uneducated; it is quite another to be near someone we perceive as unstable. Such people threaten our feelings of safety and security, much as Tom did to the person in the theater.

Beyond the fact that nonverbal communication is "read" as a reflection of our emotional state, *it is also important to realize that, unlike verbal language, nonverbal communication is continuous.* Consider the behavior of a nine-year-old boy named John:

One of our students, Sam, was sent to interview John as we watched through a one-way mirror. Sam sat across from young John, who was slouched in a chair and staring at the floor. Sam asked John several questions about how he was feeling. The little boy answered with a grunted "yes," "no," or, usually, "I don't know."

Fig. 1

Sam and John are communicating without words

As Sam continued to ask questions, John's answers became increasingly brief, if possible. Sam became stumped and came out to talk to us. Angrily, Sam said that John was just a noncommunicative child who didn't want to be helped!

Fig. 2

Sam is stumped and exasperated

Sam was correct . . . but only to a point. Certainly, John had indeed chosen to stop communicating verbally. However, John had *never* stopped communicating nonverbally. To help

Sam focus on this, we asked him if he could tell how John was feeling by merely looking at his posture? "Why, yes," was the response. "His shoulders are slumped over, and his arms are folded very tightly. He looks scared and like he doesn't think much of himself or of being here."

"What is John's face communicating?" was our next question. By the time we completed asking about the other nonverbal avenues of communication, Sam had a much fuller understanding of how John was feeling. Sam returned to the interview more sensitive and empathetic to John's plight, and he was ready to "hear" what John was saying nonverbally.

Fig. 3
Positive contact is made

Later, we pointed out to Sam how *his* nonverbal language affected those first ten minutes of the interview. Although he thought he was being empathetic and professional because of the words he used, Sam's facial expressions and posture communicated his increasing anxiety and anger to John. Which do you think John was responding to . . . Sam's professional words or the look on his face?

◆

The nonstop nature of nonverbal communication has significant implications for human interaction. Recent surveys indicate that the average person spends less than forty minutes a day in actual verbal conversation with others. But when a child is verbally silent, it doesn't mean that he or she is not saying anything. Whenever we are around others, we are communicating nonverbally whether we want to or not. And while people cannot help being affected by our facial expressions, our posture, or how close we stand to them, neither can we avoid being affected by their nonverbal behavior.

Because nonverbal communication is continuous, a nonverbal deficit will generally be more pervasive and have greater impact than would a similar verbal difficulty. For example, a child who stutters will only have difficulty communicating while actually speaking. In contrast, think of a girl who has a problem with facial expressions: she looks angry when she thinks she looks happy. Any time she is around people, her expression will be communicating the wrong message about how she really feels. Other children cannot help but respond to her as if she were upset, and a chain of negative interactions can begin and will continue as long as the girl unwittingly shows her angry face to others.

Some investigators sum up the nonstop nature of nonverbal communication by saying, *"You cannot **not** communicate nonverbally!"* Therefore, those who are adept at nonverbal language stand to gain tremendous benefits while those who use it poorly are destined to experience widespread confusion and frustration—without ever knowing the reason why!

As previously stated, most children who are having difficulties in accurately communicating nonverbally do not know it.

> R ecent surveys indicate that the average person spends less than forty minutes a day in actual verbal conversation with others, but whenever we are around others, we are communicating nonverbally whether we want to or not.

Although children who don't fit in may realize that they can't make friends easily or maintain satisfactory relationships, they are usually unaware that the source of their troubles may lie in their nonverbal communication. Therefore, children with non-verbal communication deficits continue to make the same mistakes over and over again, and since other children perceive those mistakes as an accurate reflection of the child's inner feelings, social rejection results.

We've been discussing how the nonverbal language differs from the verbal, and elaborating on the following theme: because nonverbal communication takes place out of our conscious awareness, but others subconsciously read it as a reflection of our emotions, nonverbal communication carries tremendous weight in our relationships, especially since we cannot stop it. Further, there are two more comparisons we'd like to make between verbal and nonverbal laguage, both of which bring us back to our focus on children who don't fit in.

Grammar Rules

Although the grammar of the nonverbal language is unwritten, there are still rules for its use. *Residual rules* are the nonverbal rules for any given situation, and they are only noticed when they are broken. Nowhere are they written down or formalized, yet we must follow them if we are to "fit in." As Mehrabian said, "Verbal cues are definable by an explicit dictionary and by rules of syntax, but there are only vague and informal explanations of the significance of various nonverbal behaviors." Consider, for example, elevator etiquette:

As we took our place in the elevator facing forward and watching the numbers change on the floor indicator, the elevator stopped and a mother and her little girl came in. As all good elevator crowds do, we arranged ourselves equidistantly from each other, faced forward and looked up at the blinking numbers. The little girl, however, had turned so she was facing the back of the elevator, and she was staring at us. We didn't know about anyone else, but we were made very uncomfortable by her actions, and so was her mother. Quickly, her mother told her to turn around and face the door. The little girl asked, "Why?" The mother, who could sense our anxiety, was hard pressed to come up with a logical answer. Finally she said, "Because we need to see if the door opens the right way." That answer seemed to satisfy the little girl, if not her mother, and so she turned and looked very intently at the elevator door.

◆

The little girl was the "square peg" of the moment; she had broken a residual rule.

It is difficult to be certain about how, where, and from whom we learn these rules for using proper nonverbal communication. Some nonverbal patterns may be part of our behavioral repertoire at birth. For example, blind and deaf children appear to show the appropriate facial expressions reflecting emotional states, just as their sighted and hearing peers do. These inborn behaviors are important, but most would agree that the great majority of rules are learned in other, largely informal ways. The very informality of the process, compared with the formal, school-based lessons of English grammar, often makes the learning of nonverbal skills a hit-or-miss affair in which some children have much training and others relatively little, and where great gaps in knowledge can go undetected until the resulting social problems appear "for no apparent reason." Such gaps can occur in the following six areas:

1. A child from New York City has a different "rhythm" than a child from Baton Rouge, Louisiana. Their speech patterns and attitudes are indicative of the differences in their environment. A problem arises when they are out of "sync" with one another— one child cannot adjust to the other child's rhythm. Further,

arriving on time or being late for appointments communicates our regard for another person. Time management is a nonverbal form of language that communicates caring.

2. Interpersonal distance—space—is a portable territory with boundaries that we all carry around with us. If a child stands too close to others while having a conversation, that child is violating the space rules, and is likely to be labeled as strange. However, the child is probably unaware that he or she has done anything wrong. Further, a child who touches others inappropriately, either in terms of the location or the intensity of that contact, stands an excellent chance of being viewed as frightening or weird.

3. Children need to know which gestures and postures to use and when to use them. A child may indeed speak the English verbal language perfectly well, but if he or she does not complement the words with the correct, and correctly used, gestures and postures, the child will have trouble communicating and will probably not fit in.

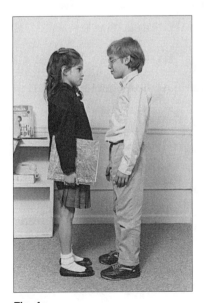

Fig. 5
Gestures and postures should
be correctly used and integrated

Fig. 4
A space rule violation

Fig. 6
Facial expressions communicate
feelings

Fig. 7
Communication through appearance

4. Effective eye contact and the appropriate use of facial expressions are the two most frequently noted characteristics of socially adept children. During a conversation, we spend about 30 to 60 percent of the time looking at the other person's face. Obviously, a child can run into trouble if he or she unknowingly uses the wrong facial expression or the correct facial expression with the wrong intensity (for example, laughing when only a smile is appropriate).

5. Paralanguage refers to all those aspects of sound which communicate emotion and are used either with words or independently. Whistling and humming are paralanguage, as are tone, intensity, and loudness of voice. Nearly one third of the emotional meaning of interpersonal conversations is carried through paralanguage. Again, its misuse can be harmful; often, something as minor as the constant clearing of one's throat can lead to social rejection.

6. Style of dress indicates that individuals are part of a group, and keeps them from being singled out as strange or different. Unfortunately, the concept of "nerd" or "loser" is all too frequently tied to the clothes a person wears and how those clothes are worn. An outfit that a child "must have" for school may be just as important as a parent's tailored suit is for the office. Further, in our society, good personal hygiene is expected and is viewed as a basic necessity for interacting with others. If a little boy repeatedly forgets to shower after baseball practice, he may well experience social rejection as a result.

Long before a parent and child are able to sit down and have a coherent verbal discussion, they will have countless opportunities for nonverbal exchanges and development. Consider Baby Andy:

The baby named Andy had just finished with his bath and his father was powdering him. As he sprinkled powder on the baby, the father was making exaggerated faces and cooing sounds. The baby was responding to these antics by making cooing sounds back, smiling and thrashing about with his arms and legs. "Whoosee little boo boo is you?" said this grown man, who is a respected scholar in his field. "Whoosee, whoosee, whoosee, whooseeee!" he continued to the seeming delight of Andy, whose own responses ignited another round of exaggerated facial expressions and nonsensical sounds from the two of them.

◆

Like verbal communications, nonverbal communications with infants, and to some extent young children as well, are characterized by a form of "baby talk." When children begin to use verbal language, adults usually try to converse with them using simple, easy-to-understand words. The same process takes place in nonverbal communication. As seen in the case above, the father is exaggerating his expression well beyond what would normally be appropriate for adult nonverbal communication. He is "talking" nonverbal baby talk.

Appropriate nonverbal "baby" communications are used by children and adults to build the relationships necessary for effective emotional development. Without such development, children may lose their way on the path to adulthood. Again, if children are not given the opportunity to learn to communicate at these more basic levels, they may be at a developmental disadvantage compared to other children who have experienced the appropriate lessons for interacting nonverbally.

Communication Deficits

If we assume that nonverbal language is as complex in its development and use as verbal language, we may also assume that it is vulnerable to the same kinds of problems. In *receptive language deficits*, children have difficulty understanding the information they *receive*. In the widely known receptive *verbal* deficit, dyslexia, children have trouble reading the words printed on a page, even though they have average or above-average intelligence. Because they don't receive information accurately, dyslexics mix up letters and words. For example, they may reverse the letters 'd' and 'b,' so that the word "dog" could be read as "bog."

*Based upon Greek roots such as those for dyslexia, we propose that a nonverbal social communication deficit might also be termed **dyssemia**, meaning a difficulty (dys) in using nonverbal signs or signals (semes).*

Paralleling receptive language problems are *expressive verbal language deficits*. In deficits of this type, children have trouble *expressing or producing* verbal information. For example, a child might read the word "may" correctly, but when he or she attempts to write or articulate "may," "yam" is produced instead. Expressive verbal problems can be severely debilitating, like receptive deficits, and have been the subject of much research.

These verbal deficits have, we believe, mirror images—parallels—in the nonverbal domain. In much the same way that dyslexics have difficulty with the written word (*dys* = difficulty, *lexic* = words), many socially rejected children cannot understand or "read" the quieter messages of others. Using Greek roots such as those for dyslexia, we propose that a nonverbal social communication deficit might be termed *dyssemia*, meaning a difficulty (*dys*) in using nonverbal signs or signals (*semes*). For example, a person with receptive facial dyssemia may misread a happy face as an angry one and as a result may return a smile with a frown or glare. This is not the stuff comfortable relationships are built on!

Thus, dyssemic children can have trouble using nonverbal language. Consider how an expressive deficit affected two elementary school girls, Karen and Sara:

Karen, who has an expressive, not receptive, dyssemia, has no trouble accurately understanding Sara's smile, and decides to send back one of her own. However, because she has a deficit in using her face to express her feelings, Karen unknowingly puts on an angry face instead. You can imagine how the rest of this sequence will probably go. Sara will wonder what she did to make Karen angry, and will probably then look bewildered. Karen, who can accurately read this, will be equally confused as to why her attempt at returned friendliness was not accepted. Although both girls would like to be friends, the chances of that happening are diminishing rapidly.

◆

Just as it is possible to have more than one kind of verbal language deficit, a child can have multiple nonverbal language difficulties as well. Life for these children must be a continual jumble of unforeseen reactions and confusing counter reactions.

It's no wonder that some of them may choose to retreat from contact and remain alone.

What You Can Do to Help

If you suspect that your child is dyssemic—suffering from a nonverbal communication deficit—there are steps you can take to help, and our purpose in writing this book is to show you how to do that. In the following pages, we will guide you through the processes of assessing your child's nonverbal communication skills and then correcting any problems you discover.

1. Laying Out the Puzzle Pieces: Assessment

If you accurately assess your child's problem, you can remedy the problem more efficiently and effectively. *Remember, accurate assessment saves both time and effort.* Fortunately, you **do not** need to have extensive professional training to do an effective informal assessment of your child's nonverbal language abilities. Indeed, the first and most important tool of assessment is awareness. We believe that if you become aware of the nonverbal language, you will be able to consciously observe what you normally do not see. Then, you will be in a good position to use your common sense to evaluate whether or not your child has a problem.

In the following chapters, we will describe in fuller detail the six channels of nonverbal communication:

> 1. **rhythm and the use of time,**
> 2. **interpersonal distance (space) and touch,**
> 3. **gestures and postures,**
> 4. **facial expressions,**
> 5. **paralinguistics (voice tone, pitch, etc.),**
> 6. **objectics (style of dress).**

Once you become more consciously aware of these six components, you will have gone a long way toward being able to assess many problems that a child might have in these areas. Indeed, you may be able to assess the child's nonverbal functioning simply by observing him or her. Or you may find it necessary to go through some of the more formal assessment procedures we'll describe. In either case, it is very important to let the child know what is going on. Since many of the child's interpersonal problems are likely to stem from events that he or she is unaware of, you want to make the child directly aware of what you are doing. *Form a partnership; be a tutor.* The more you can build a cooperative, supportive relationship with the child, the better. *These children need to be reassured.* To accomplish this, discuss openly what you are trying to assess; explain that you understand how confusing school and friends can be, and assure the child that you want to help figure out what might be causing the bad times.

Fig. 8
Discuss openly
what you are
trying to assess

With a positive relationship that ensures and maintains privacy (when needed), you and the child can try a number of general, informal assessment approaches. Using a little ingenuity, you can make the assessment pleasant and gamelike. In assessing *receptive* abilities, the television, for example, is one simple, useful informal assessment device that children will accept with little or no anxiety.

Only your imagination limits your use of television for informal nonverbal language assessment. Once you have found a satisfactory program showing substantial interactions among children and adults (we have found "Sesame Street" and various daytime dramas to be good choices), turn off the sound and have the child tell you what is going on by simply watching the picture. Every so often turn up the volume to check the child's accuracy. Focus on the different types of nonverbal communication separately and in combination with each other: facial expressions, postures, gestures, clothing and the like. Conversely, you can darken the picture and have the child listen to the sound and make guesses about what is going on visually. These are just some of the fun, easy ways to use television to find out how adept your child is at reading nonverbal cues. Further tips regarding television use are provided in Part Two.

Similar assessments of receptive skills can be made by observing people in various places and asking the child to tell you what he or she thinks is going on. For example, shopping malls are wonderful places to watch numerous interactions and to test a child's ability to tell what is happening—which will tell you how adept that child is at reading nonverbal social information. Have your child watch people sitting in food courts or restaurants; see if the child can guess how those people are feeling and what their relationships are. You can also view groups of individuals as they move through the mall and ask the child to explain what, if any, relationships these people share.

When it comes to assessing *expressive* nonverbal abilities, you may be faced with an even easier task than assessing the receptive ones. The most important thing here is for you to be aware of how your child *sends* nonverbal language signals. There are many opportunities to watch your child interact with others or respond to events (birthday parties, arguments between children, viewing an exciting sports event, movie or television show). Given the situation, you can know rather easily what kinds of feelings are probably being experienced by the child, so you can assess whether the child is accurately expressing those feelings. Through such observations, you will become aware of how easy or difficult it is for others to accurately interpret how the child is feeling. If you are having trouble reading the child's emotions, chances are that others are, too. Or, if you find that the child's nonverbal language does not reflect his or her probable internal state—if the child looks mad while actually having a good time at a birthday party, for example—you will know that others are likely to misinterpret the child's facial expressions.

If you have an instant photo camera or a videorecorder, you can be a bit more systematic about your observations. You can ask your child to show certain emotions and record his or her attempts; this photographic record can help you confirm whether there are difficulties in expressing feelings nonverbally. Remember, however, that this kind of technique is *reactive*—that is, children will react to being photographed and may not show the kind of nonverbal communications that they usually do because they may be "camera shy." Try to reduce this possibility by having the child also take pictures of you, or make the picture-taking part of a game, perhaps with a group of children. Or, photograph the child when he or she is unaware that you are doing so, perhaps on the playground or at a party. These general observational assessments will help you evaluate your child's nonverbal communication processing abilities.

Before we move on, we want to alert you to some characteristics often found in children with nonverbal social communication deficits. First, it is important to realize that these dyssemic children generally want to participate with others in play or in family activities; they do not choose to be alone, nor do they seek rejection. They want to get along with others and go along with what is expected of them, although that is not always reflected in their behavior.

Here are additional indicators of dyssemia, taken from Doris Johnson and Helmer Myklebust and other researchers. The child:

- is often described by parents and teachers as tactless and insensitive

- is often described by other children as "dumb" but usually is average or above average in intelligence

- is often described by parents as being "different" since infancy

- is often seen by parents and teachers as "lacking in social maturity"

- often has difficulty perceiving danger

- often has difficulty understanding when something is a hazard

- often has difficulty understanding rules and sequences of games

- often has difficulty recognizing the contingency between his or her behavior and the consequences of that behavior

- often feels some or all of the following: sad, bewildered, lonely, confused, anxious, and different

◆ often perseveres in action or activity even when it leads to punishment or failure

■ is inconsistent; will be accurate in one form of nonverbal communication one day but not the next.

There is no firm number of indicators for defining when a child may be dyssemic. The greater the number of indicators, however, the more likely it is that the child is having significant difficulty processing nonverbal social information. Again, further information and tips to help you with assessment are provided throughout the rest of the text: the following chapters will give you the foundation to conduct an informal assessment, and in Part Two we'll describe formal assessment.

*T*he greater the number of indicators, the more likely it is that the child is having signifi-cant difficulty processing nonver-bal information.

2. Solving the Puzzle: Remediation

Once you have determined what problem or problems your child has in communicating nonverbally, you can determine how to improve the child's nonverbal skills. For some children, infor-mal, short-term intervention may be all that is necessary to head them in the right direction. This is the possibility we'll examine throughout Part One. As we describe the six areas of nonverbal communication, we'll also give you tips on how to remedy problems in these areas. These tips can be used on an as-needed basis, and many of them involve the same aids we recommend for the assessment process: trips to shopping malls, use of TV and videotapes, etc. As with assessment, too, the remediation pro-cedures offered in the upcoming chapters should be performed in an atmosphere of partnership, cooperation, and fun, and you should be sure to make the child aware of what you are doing and why.

For some children, more extensive, formalized, and continuous help may be needed. If, for example, the evaluation shows that a child has general problems in reading *and* sending several kinds of nonverbal messages, then a broad, intensive remediation approach is required. Part Two will discuss formal and informal approaches to remediation, and will also provide some further insights as to the physical and emotional causes of nonverbal communication deficits.

CHAPTER ONE:

SETTING THE PACE: RHYTHM AND THE USE OF TIME

SETTING THE PACE: RHYTHM AND THE USE OF TIME

◇

In the introduction, we said that although verbal language is formally taught in school, there are no textbooks for nonverbal language. It seems that children are expected to somehow absorb nonverbal language, to learn the rules indirectly. We will now attempt to define the nonverbal "grammar," and make it less mysterious. We will begin with those nonverbal behaviors that we are typically unaware of, and will move toward the behaviors that we can monitor more easily. We'll start with what may be the most basic forms of nonverbal communication, rhythm and the use of time.

Have you ever been far from home and met someone with whom you just clicked—really liked—only to find out later that he or she was from your region of the country? The compatibility results, in part, because the two of you share the same *rhythm* or *pace of life*, a pattern that is very basic and learned very early.

Perhaps you've also experienced the opposite situation. We have. One of us grew up in Wisconsin and the other in New Jersey. For years, the Wisconsinite felt rushed by the Jerseyite, while the Jerseyite was frustrated by what he saw as the Midwesterner's slow, methodical approach to just about everything. When we would attend conferences in the Midwest, one of us always felt "right at home," while the other was uneasy. However, the situation was reversed when we attended professional meetings in New York. There, one was comfortable with the chaotic and hectic pace, while the other was made anxious by it.

Such experiences reflect the possibility that rhythmic differences can play an important part in interpersonal relationships. Consider Nick and his family.

Nick was the second of three children; his older brother and younger sister were the biological children of his parents. Nick, however, had been adopted when he was a baby. While his siblings were doing well academically and socially, Nick seemed to be troubled. He always felt "out of sync" with his family; as we observed his family in its daily functioning, we saw that Nick actually was out of sync. At the dinner table, while his parents and siblings ate quickly, Nick ate very slowly; inevitably, the family became impatient while waiting for him to finish. This problem became especially acute on trips, when stopping at fast food restaurants on the highway. In addition to the problem at mealtimes, Nick dressed more slowly than everyone else and always seemed to be late.

Nick's emotional rhythm also seemed aberrant. While his family was quite emotional and reacted strongly to situations, Nick's reactions were moderate. His parents often misinterpreted this different level of responsiveness as an indication that he did not care about things that they cared about. Although he tried as hard as he could, Nick could not match his rhythm to theirs; the result was a degree of tension and misunderstanding that led the family to seek professional help.

◆

Being out of sync with others can make a child feel anxious and uncomfortable. However, there are some people, among them some remarkably successful adults, who can accurately "read" and then synchronize their own rhythms to those of others. Pat, for instance, knows how to set the pace with children and adults.

Pat, a very effective elementary school teacher, was on a playground with a number of children. When she was with a child who walked or ran rapidly, she matched that child's pace; when with a slower child, she did the same. Pat made each child comfortable with her rhythm. Regardless of the child's gender, social or ethnic background, or daily mood, she communicated her understanding of that child through her nonverbal behavior. Further, Pat was always able to finish her meal at the same time as her colleagues. While they rarely could say why, people were at ease around Pat.

◆

As you can see, rhythms can play powerful roles in social rejection or success. The skill of using rhythms, however, appears to have two components. First, a child must learn to recognize the rhythms of others, and know what they mean. This is **receptive rhythm usage.** Second, he or she must have the flexibility to adjust his or her own rhythms to match those of others. This is **expressive rhythm usage.** A child may suffer from rhythm dyssemia if these skills are not developed. Because of her receptive rhythm dyssemia, Robyn had trouble at home.

Robyn was a twelve-year-old whose problems with the receptive use of rhythms caused great stress for her and her family. A sweet and affable girl, Robyn would nevertheless become embroiled in family squabbles whenever her parents were in a hurry. As do most people, Robyn's parents would begin to move a bit faster when they were short of time. Robyn's two older brothers had little trouble picking up these cues from

31

their parents and speeded up their activites accordingly. However, we observed that Robyn did not pick up on her parents increased speed of movement, and she typically continued to move at her usually adaptive, moderate daily pace. Inevitably, this led to criticism from her parents and jibes from her brothers about being a "slow poke." Once Robyn was made aware of how behavioral rhythms can vary at different points in the day and under differing circumstances, the family's difficulties abated significantly.

◆

Several of the tips presented later in this section are aimed at nurturing these abilities, which Sean, a sixteen-year-old student leader in an inner city high school, used remarkably well.

There was a good reason why Sean became the president of the student government association. The school, located downtown in a large city, served a multicultural population. Sean was able to get along well with everyone because of what his teachers described as his amazing ability to adapt himself to any group. When Sean met with Oriental students, he acted very differently than when he was talking with Indian or Pakistani youngsters. Specifically, he could "read" the rhythms of each group—how quickly or slowly they liked to talk and decide things—and he could then adjust his pace to match theirs. Sean inevitably won school elections. More students felt comfortable with and understood by him than by any other candidate. His excellent understanding of the expressive use of nonverbal rhythms contributed significantly to Sean's success.

◆

In addition to being aware of personal and cultural rhythms in the way Sean and Pat did, it is also important, when working with children, to keep their natural rhythms in mind. Many parents report that changes in rhythm strongly affect their youngsters. If a child is used to getting nine hours of sleep and only gets seven; if he or she gets up late or is unable to have breakfast; if daylight savings time is imposed and the child has to get up an hour earlier—the child's rhythm may be affected and thus the child may be less interpersonally effective. While most children will adjust to rhythm shifts after a few days, an awareness of these shifts can often help parents and teachers to reduce or minimize potential problems.

> **B**eing out of sync with others can make a child feel anxious and uncomfortable.

Another way parents and teachers can apply their knowledge of rhythm is to plan the toughest activities for times when they and the children are at their best. Sometimes this is not possible, but even so, most teachers know that difficult subjects should only be taught at certain times of day when children are at their sharpest. This is a simple but important way to make use of your knowledge of personal and natural rhythms.

■ TIPS FOR PARENTS AND TEACHERS ■
Helping Children with Rhythm Dyssemia

1. Vary your rate of hand clapping and ask the child to stay with you as you change from one rate to another.

☐

2. Have the child practice speaking, playing, or writing at different speeds.

☐

3. Use the second hand on a clock to guide the child's rate of questioning or responding to questions.

☐

4. Have the child estimate the passage of various amounts of time. For example, ask him or her to tell you when thirty seconds or one minute has passed.

☐

5. Have your child observe the rates of various behaviors in others and try to parallel those rates. For example, have him or her swing at the same pace as another child on a swingset.

☐

6. Describe situations in which it would be appropriate for the child to slow or increase the speed of behavior, and ask him or her to role play in such situations. You might also use photos or cut-outs from magazines that depict such situations. An example would be a scene showing a person trying to catch a train or plane when time is short, or a situation in which there is a long line waiting to get into a movie theater.

□

Perfect Timing

Rhythms are aspects of time usage that are present from birth, but as we grow older, we are more able to control our use or *misuse* of time. For children as well as adults, the ways in which we organize our time and meet our commitments can say a great deal to others. Conversely, people tell us a great deal about their feelings for us through their use, abuse, or respect for our time.

Our verbal language reflects how important time is to us. *It's time! Having the time of our lives! Time flies when you're having fun. Doing time. Time sharing. Time out.* The list could go on and on, but the point is that time is important to us, and yet, as with other nonverbal language, we often forget its communicative importance until someone breaks a time rule.

Punctuality can have communicative value. One of our sons found this out during a school break when he applied for a summer job with a temporary employment agency. He left in plenty of time to arrive promptly, but he took a wrong turn. Finding himself lost with just two minutes until his appointment, he stopped at a pay phone and called the agency. Upon explaining that he would be a few minutes late, he was told, "Don't bother, you are not the kind of person we are looking for." How many of us have been kept waiting by someone

> To say that our friends and family are important to us means little if we do not spend a significant portion of our available time with them. Thus, time is one way we communicate caring.

and have perceived that person to be uncaring, self-centered, and irresponsible? The ability to be on time is seen by many as a responsibility and a desirable quality.

Expressive time usage describes the behavior in which we say something to others through the use of time. We can tell others that they are very important to us by spending time with them or by waiting for them if they are delayed. To say that our friends and family are important to us means little if we do not spend a significant portion of our available time with them. *Thus, time is one way we communicate caring.*

We also can demonstrate respect for others by the use of time; the time we are willing to wait for someone can be directly related to the status of the person involved. For example, anyone who has ever been to a physician's office learns what waiting for a high-status person is all about.

As with all nonverbal communication, culture plays an important part in the communicative meaning of time. Just as rhythm varies in different regions of the United States, so the meaning of time varies with culture; it is important to recognize this in order to prevent miscommunication. In our culture, "time is money," and many say, "Why put off till tomorrow what you can do today?" There is a reason why fast food establishments got their start here. However, we must realize that not all cultures and people share our view that lunch is something to finish as quickly as possible.

Significant misunderstandings can develop if time cues are misread or misexpressed. For instance, if you are invited to a party that goes from 7:00 P.M. until 9:00 P.M., when should you arrive? According to Judee Burgoon and Thomas Saine, two researchers in the nonverbal language area, it depends on which part of the country you are from. If you are in New York or Chicago, anytime from 8:00 P.M. on is acceptable, but never right at 7:00 P.M. However, if you are in Salt Lake City or a small town in the South, you should arrive as close to 7:00 P.M. as possible without being early. In one instance, arriving on time would be rude; in the other, arriving late would be inexcusable.

Clearly, the communicative use of time can be a powerful factor in social success. In the case of a twelve-year-old named Rob, it proved to be his undoing. His story may be a familiar one.

Rob's problem was simple; he could not organize his time well enough to do all the things he needed or committed himself to do. He said he would be places and he wasn't. His teachers and peers became irate. Rob would say that he would be somewhere in fifteen minutes and would show up forty-five minutes later; he would say something would be done in two days and it would take four. Everyone was continually irritated by his broken promises. Rob could not judge time, and he did not realize its communicative value to others. As a result, his was a story of failure in interpersonal relationships. He meant well but was unaware of the reason why things came apart.

◆

The flip side of the expressive use of time is **receptive time usage.** This involves understanding the way others use time to communicate, and it is also an important factor in social success. Time cues are an important source of interpersonal information. For example, a child must learn that if a teacher says a homework assignment requires two hours to complete, it should not be glossed over in a few minutes; it is "serious" homework. Similarly, if a child is told to be in the principal's office at 10:00 A.M., the child should realize that if the principal has not appeared by 10:10, the waiting should continue. Sensitivity to the meaning of time factors is a very subtle skill, but it's a skill that socially successful people seem to have mastered. Such people are aware that social and academic interactions take place in time, and they use this awareness to achieve their interpersonal goals.

The accurate reading and expressing of time information can often spell the difference between success and failure in a relationship. As in the case of rhythms, skill in time usage is composed of various abilities. For example, we should be able to arrive promptly for appointments. This is a skill that takes much practice, but it is an especially important skill in our culture. In the United States, perhaps the most crucial feature of time usage is the ability to be *on time.* Some people consider punctuality to be a bother and are notoriously late for things. Those of us who know such people often resent them. Therefore, they are often rejected or avoided, and they simply don't know why.

■ TIPS FOR PARENTS AND TEACHERS ■
Helping a Child Develop Better Time Skills

1. Have your child keep track of the number of times he or she is late for something as compared to being on time or even early. Have the child chart the progress as he or she tries to improve from week to week.

☐

2. Practice time estimation. Give the child a variety of tasks and assignments, and ask for an estimate of how long it will take to complete them. Prepare a reward system in which he or she receives points and such for accurate estimates. Give bonus points for improved time estimation from week to week.

☐

3. Teach ways of estimating accurate "travel" times. Describe some places that your child must go and provide a target time for his or her arrival. Ask the child not only to tell you how long it should take to get to the destination but also what time it is necessary to start the journey in order to arrive on time. If the child has difficulties, provide some tips such as overestimating to arrive a bit early. Use a progress chart to keep track of and illuminate the child's improvement.

☐

4. Provide the child with an inexpensive watch that has a built-in stopwatch. Teach him or her how to set the watch for a "time for task" or "time for travel" estimation.

Demonstrate how the watch can then be used to guide the speed of working or walking, etc.

☐

5. Discuss the possible meanings of punctuality. What does being late mean to a friend who is waiting for you? How is this different from keeping your teacher waiting? Your school principal? Your physician? Your grandparent? How does the child feel when he or she is kept waiting by various kinds of people?

☐

6. Present scenarios in which adults or other children either do or do not control their time effectively. Explain how the outcomes of the stories could have changed if time communication had been different.

☐

7. Have your child keep track of the punctuality and use of time by others, such as parents, teachers, or peers.

☐

Rhythm and the use of time as forms of communication are things that we can easily ignore; they seem so obvious and insignificant. However, it has been our repeated experience that these components of nonverbal language, being so basic, can have dramatic impacts, both good and bad, on our well-being. Parents and teachers who help children to develop skills in these areas are helping to build a crucial foundation upon which interpersonal success may later rest.

CHAPTER TWO:

OUT OF BOUNDS: USE OF SPACE AND TOUCH

OUT OF BOUNDS: USE OF SPACE AND TOUCH

◇

Most animals are territorial. We can watch them set boundaries around their dens or nests, and they will defend this space if necessary. As you may know, dogs often "mark" their territories (both outside and inside the house) so that other animals will stay away. For dogs, and other animals, territory is defined on the basis of specific odors. For humans, however, territory might be delineated with other concrete indicators such as signs and fences.

There are other examples which illustrate human territoriality. The popular sports of football, soccer, and basketball are territorial games in which the main objective is to violate or defend a territory. We are especially territorial about where we live. Imagine that you are at home and looking out your window at the street in front of your house. So long as the cars keep moving past, you are comfortable, but should a car stop in front of your house, you become more attentive and watch what is happening more closely. Similarly, if a person is walking on the sidewalk in front of your house, everything is fine, but should that person step onto your lawn and move closer to your home, you again become attentive and perhaps even tense. Clearly our territory is important to us.

In relation to nonverbal language, our *personal space* is more important than our *territorial space*—the structures which we inhabit. *Personal space* refers to a portable territory we all carry around with us. As depicted in figure 2.1, personal space may be seen as a flexible bubble that surrounds us. The bubble is wider in the back than in the front and contracts or expands depending on the situation. Children and adults who have trouble defining that bubble may have spatial or territorial dyssemia.

The diagram in figure 2.2 is based upon the research done by Edward T. Hall using American subjects. It shows that inside this bubble there are four zones within which it is appropriate for particular kinds of communication to take place. The first of these areas is called the *intimate zone,* wherein we permit close friends and family to relate to us and where we allow the discussion of intimate issues and feelings. It begins at nearly touching and extends out about eighteen inches or so. Next, we come to the *personal zone,* extending from about eighteen inches to four feet. This is the distance within which we conduct conversations with friends and acquaintances in the majority of everyday settings. The third area is called the *social zone,* which ranges from four to approximately twelve feet; it is appropriate to talk loudly in this zone so that those with whom we have just met or are about to meet can hear us. Because there is a good chance that others can see what is taking place in the social zone, intimate, personal, and other private matters are not supposed to be discussed there. The final area, called the *public zone,* encompasses the largest amount of space, starting at twelve feet and ranging to infinity. We do not typically talk to people who are this far away from us; although we may see people who are in our public zone, we can only communicate with them through postures and gestures until they approach our social zone.

While all people have a bubble of personal space surrounding them, the size and importance of the various zones changes dramatically from culture to culture. When people of different cultures interact, they often have difficulties in negotiating a com-

P *ersonal space refers to a portable territory we all carry around with us.*

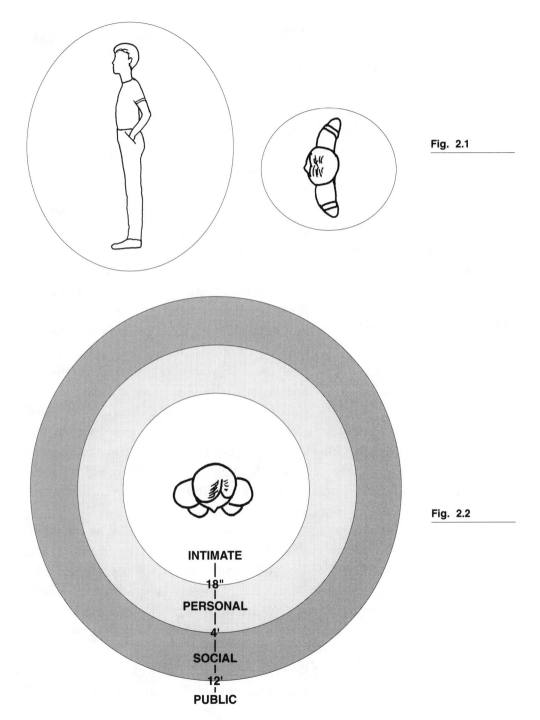

Fig. 2.1

Fig. 2.2

INTIMATE
18"
PERSONAL
4'
SOCIAL
12'
PUBLIC

fortable space. It is important to be aware of the intimate, personal, social, and public zones of people from other cultures so that we do not inadvertently break a personal space rule when we are with them.

Spatial dyssemia can occur even between people of the same culture. Violating someone's space is a residual rule violation. Most of us know people who stand too close to us while talking; they make us very uncomfortable and we tend to pull back and avoid them. According to Hall, these people are using the intimate zone for conversations that should take place in the personal zone. Or, there are people who talk too loudly at the social zone distance about things that more properly are discussed within the relative privacy of the intimate zone. For example, we knew a teenager whose mother frequently discussed family matters at a social zone distance, thus allowing others to overhear and causing the youngster intense stress and discomfort. Finally, moving further out into the public zone, there are people who, thirty feet or so away, will call out loudly, "Hi! How are you doing?" If you are like most people, you will react to this with some discomfort and will try to find some way to avoid answering until reaching the social zone distance of twelve feet.

While it is common for very young children to violate the personal space of others, they have to learn quickly where their space ends and that of others begins.

It is amazing to realize how many space rules we must know and follow everyday. As long as we follow these rules, we are accepted and people feel comfortable with us; as soon as we violate a simple rule of space usage, however, we risk the possibility of being labeled as weird or being rejected by others. By the time we are adults, we are expected to know the necessary rules for managing personal space.

Although children are given more leeway for space mistakes than adolescents and adults, they still can experience social rejection if they do not "obey the rules." We are indebted to the teachers with whom we have worked for giving us cogent examples of what one of them called "space invaders." While it is common for very young children to violate the personal space of others, they have to learn quickly where their space ends and that of others begins. For some children, learning this is difficult; they drop things under the chairs of neighboring children, and without saying the appropriate "excuse me," or "do you mind?" violate another's space—an action that usually causes some kind of altercation. You may think that a child should know about the spatial zones intuitively, but this is not the case, for *spatial zones are taught through nonverbal communication.* Apparently, Jason failed to learn them and developed **receptive spatial dyssemia.**

A teacher reported that many of the conflicts and fights involving six-year-old Jason could be traced to the fact that he had little awareness of proper space usage. When working with other children at a large table, he spread his papers far beyond his "area" and well into the "territories" of others. When they pushed his materials back toward him, he would become angry and go after them physically. The same pattern was observed while the children were waiting in line to go to the lunch room. Whereas the other children were careful to allow some space to exist between themselves and others, Jason was inevitably pushing himself forward into someone or leaning backward into someone else. The result was the same as at the work table—pushing and shoving followed by fighting. Each time, Jason complained that he was the victim and that other children pushed him first. He clearly did not understand that he had started these fights because he was a "space invader."

◆

Consider how *verbal* language affects personal space usage. Had Jason learned to say "excuse me" when he inadvertently violated the space of another, he would have experienced far fewer conflicts. We need to say "excuse me" when we enter another's personal space, especially the intimate zone. Why? Because we are breaking a residual rule of personal space usage and are asking forgiveness in advance.

Jason probably would have been helped by a tip that a very creative teacher gave to us. She helped children get a concrete sense of their own personal space by placing masking tape around their chairs and between children who shared tables. This made what most children already knew obvious and observable to others, and the interpersonal problems caused by violations of personal space all but disappeared.

Mark was a ten-year-old who experienced both **receptive** and **expressive spatial dyssemia.**

Mark was ridiculed by some children and avoided by most. After extensive classroom observation, it was noted that he had great difficulty with the language of space. He stood too close to others when he spoke; when sitting at a shared table, he spread his books and materials out too far; he constantly let his chair bump into that of his neighbor. Mark seemed totally unaware that he was breaking any number of residual rules of space usage, and that he was alienating himself from others through his violation of their space.

In addition to his expressive difficulties with personal space, Mark also had trouble reading the space cues sent by other people. When out on the playground, he was typically off by himself. However, when asked with whom he was playing, he would indicate another child or group of children well beyond his personal or social zones. The same was true of children he called friends; none appeared within his personal or intimate zones during the day. Mark was unable to "read" what others' use of space was telling him—in this case, that he had no friends or playmates. Mark's misuse and misinterpretation of territoriality played a large part in his social difficulties.

◆

We think there is a good chance that you already know a few people who misuse or misread space cues, and the group certainly is not limited to children. These individuals typically mean well and want to be accepted by others, but are quite confused when others seem to avoid them. They are among the most poignant examples of the adverse effects of dyssemia as they encounter failure after failure in their struggle for acceptance. On the bright side, however, it has been our experience to see positive changes in both the self-confidence and relationships of individuals who are made aware of the spatial cues and rules.

■ TIPS FOR PARENTS AND TEACHERS ■
Helping Your Child Watch His or Her Distance

1. The most basic ability is to be aware of space variation. To develop this awareness, have the child observe people sitting on park benches or sofas or standing in line for lunch; point out that, unless there is a good reason to do so, they are not touching each other. Watch for birds on telephone wires; point out their use of space. Observe children in class photos or some other circumstance; point out the proper interpersonal distances between them. Watch for the use or misuse of space in TV shows and movies, or the interaction of other people in malls, at school, and other public places.

☐

2. Teach your child how to estimate and maintain proper space. While working one-on-one with the child, first allow him or her to establish a comfortable and appropriate distance. Then shift your position either closer or further away and ask the child to readjust as well. Do this several times, role-playing different situations (pretend you're at the park, a mall, at home).

☐

3. Have several children seated on movable chairs in a circle or at a table. Have another child enter the group with a chair of his or her own. Help the children to see how each must adjust space usage to accommodate the additional child. Practice this with the new person being

USE OF SPACE AND TOUCH

a teacher, a parent, an elderly person, etc., and discuss how the person's identity changes the children's responses.

☐

4. Set out a six-foot strip of masking tape on the floor. Have your child stand at one end of it and describe some imaginary people standing at the other end. Ask him or her to walk toward the "other" and to stop where he or she thinks it would be appropriate. Include among the "imaginaries" parents, siblings, teachers, police officers, principals, friends, enemies, strangers, etc. This will make the child aware that variations are needed, and should also teach the child to use appropriate distances.

☐

5. Using the same strip of tape, ask the child to remain stationary, and adopting various roles, pretend you are approaching him or her. Help the child to "read" the situation effectively. That is, is this a friendly, safe situation or do you need to be careful? Is this person someone who wants to play with you or not? Some examples would be having a stranger stop very close to the child or having a peer stop far away.

☐

The sense of touch

How important is touch? Investigators Ronald Adler and Neil Towne think it may be the difference between life and death:

> Besides being the earliest means we have of making contact with others, touching is essential to our healthy development. During the nineteenth and early twentieth centuries, a large percentage of children born every year died from a disease called marasmus, which, translated from the Greek, means, 'washing away.' In some orphanages the mortality rate was nearly one hundred percent, but even children from the most "progressive" homes, hospitals and other institutions died regularly from the ailment. . . . They hadn't been touched enough, and as a result they died. (pp. 225–6)

Just receiving the biological essentials for life isn't enough. We need more. We need to be touched and held in order to know we are loved. There are some who have even suggested that many Americans who suffer from touch deprivation turn to substitutes such as drugs and alcohol to fill the void.

To understand the importance of touch, we must realize that it anchors one end of the personal space dimension; it is zero interpersonal distance. As with personal space usage, there are extensive cultural differences regarding rules of touch. According to studies of different cultures, we in the United States are among the least prone to touch or be touched. In fact, of all the countries of the world, only the British prefer to touch and be touched less than we do.

An interesting study of contrasting cultural touch behaviors was conducted by Sidney Jourard. He observed the number of touches per hour that took place between couples in cafes in four different locations: Gainesville, Florida; London, England; Paris, France; and San Juan, Puerto Rico. Consistent with what we know about cultural differences in touch, couples in the United States averaged only two contacts compared to 180 and 110 touches for couples in Puerto Rico and France, respectively. Only the English couples touched less than those in the United States; in fact, they didn't touch at all.

Most Americans are probably quite content to keep their personal space relatively large and to have that space violated as seldom as possible. Based on what we have said about violations of residual rules, it should come as no surprise that anyone who touches us inappropriately, in terms of either the location or the intensity of that contact, stands an excellent chance of being viewed as strange and frightening. As an example of how intricate and refined the touching rules are, consider the following situation. You are standing behind someone who is involved in some activity. You do not know the person's name. How do you get his or her attention? Most people give us the same answer. They would tap the person very lightly on the shoulder and say "excuse me." Further, the tap must be made very lightly and on about a one-inch-square place on the shoulder equidistant from the neck and the end of the shoulder—and the person doing the tapping must say "excuse me." Any variance from this strict procedure will probably startle and frighten the person being tapped.

> *It should come as no surprise that anyone who touches us inappropriately, in terms of either the location or the intensity of that contact, stands an excellent chance of being viewed as strange and frightening.*

Why must we always touch people on the shoulder in this way? Because it is the rule! Why do we have to say "excuse me"? Because in order to touch someone, especially from behind, we have to violate that individual's personal space. Consider people who do not learn this basic rule. Imagine your reaction if someone attempted to get your attention by touching you on the abdomen or the side of your neck. What if you were touched in the correct place on the shoulder, but with considerable force? In any of these situations your reaction would be negative.

Other rules may not be as stringent as the shoulder touch rule is, but their violation can still bring negative reactions. Although we don't know all the rules, we, along with Jourard, have attempted to clarify some of the important ones. This research generally involved silhouette drawings of males and females, varying in age and identity. The subjects were asked where it would be acceptable to touch a particular person. The silhouettes (an example of one is provided in figure 2.3) were described as being parents, siblings, girl and boy friends, and spouses. The responses showed that most subjects agreed on where it is proper to touch and not to touch the silhouettes of different people. However, there were some subjects who did not seem to understand the

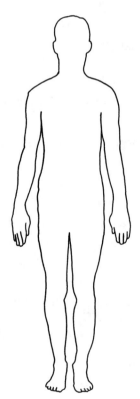

Fig. 2.3

proper vocabulary of touch and indicated they would touch areas of the body that most others would not. These subjects have problems with **expressive touch usage**—they don't know how to use the rules of touch.

Some errors of touching are more severe than others. Touching sexual areas, especially by someone who is above the age of eight, is considered an especially significant violation. In addition to there being certain "taboo" areas for touching, there are also certain body parts that are only touched under certain circumstances, and then, with great meaning attached. Research, using the silhouettes we have described, has shown that it is acceptable to touch others along the outside of their bodyline—that is, the outside of arms, the outside of legs, and so forth. In contrast to the relatively harmless touching that takes place on the outside of the bodyline, touching on the inside of the bodyline is emotion-laden. These areas include the inside of our arms and the sides of our chest and inside our legs and thighs.

Clearly, differentiating between the inside and outside of the bodyline is important. Misunderstanding touch can cause inappropriate responses in various situations. In figures 2.4 and 2.5, a boy is being escorted to the principal's office. Note that in figure 2.4 the teacher's hand is on the outside of the child's arm in a guiding position, which suggests that she has positive feelings about the young man. In figure 2.5, the teacher is escorting the boy in a different way; note that here she has violated the child's inner bodyline by using a firm grip on his arm. The meaning of this grip should be clear—the young man is in trouble. If this boy is thinking, "Hey, I'm going to the principal's office to get some kind of an award!" he has a problem with receptive touch usage—he doesn't know how to interpret others' use of touch, and in this case he will be in for a big surprise!

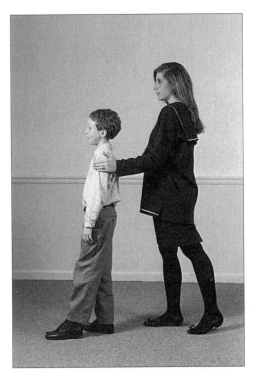

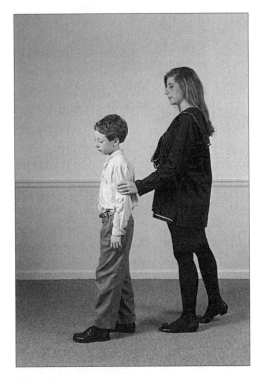

Fig. 2.4
The teacher is guiding
the boy

Fig. 2.5
The teacher's grip violates
the boy's inner bodyline

Not only can we make errors in where we touch others, but we can also make errors in how we touch them. There are many different kinds of touch, ranging from patting and squeezing to brushing and stroking. Each kind of touch communicates its own message. For example, one rarely pats someone or gets patted unless something positive is being communicated. In contrast, a squeeze can be either positive or negative depending on the circumstance. The poke, however, is almost always negative, but is especially negative when certain parts of the body are poked. This is illustrated by figure 2. 6. Note that the young man on the left is touching the upper chest area of the other boy; he is using his extended index finger in a repeated back and forth poking movement. Just looking at this picture gives the impression that an intense confrontation is imminent. There is a good reason. When you refer to yourself, where does your hand go? Most people would say that it usually goes directly to the spot being poked in the photograph. In this instance, the touch that can cause such great anger is directed at the spot which represents the essence of the other person. Would a similar reaction follow the touching of someone's forearm? We don't think so.

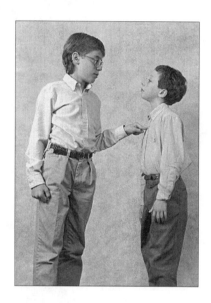

Fig. 2.6
The poke usually communicates a negative message

There are many children who suffer from the **receptive** form of touch dyssemias; the problem can be especially extreme in children who are severely emotionally disturbed. Some of these children will not allow others to touch them at all. Any attempt to provide a hug or a caring pat is quickly met with physical withdrawal. These "touch resistant" children never allow themselves to experience the benefits that can be derived from supportive contact of others. At the other extreme are children with **expressive** touch dyssemia, who cannot keep their hands to themselves and who touch others (and in some cases even themselves) inappropriately. They hug and caress people they may not even know or sit so close to strangers that their bodies are in constant contact with them. Although they may mean well, these children often are perceived by others as strange or goofy and are avoided or rejected, just like Brad.

Everybody knew Brad. When we told his teacher that we were visiting the school to observe him, her response was, "It's about time someone did something about him." As we sat in the back of the auditorium during morning assembly, we saw what she meant. Brad sat in the front row, one seat away from the teacher. Within thirty seconds his arm was around the child sitting next to him, and within five more seconds the child was complaining to his teacher. The teacher told Brad to "keep his hands to himself," and he looked embarrassed. However, within another thirty seconds, Brad was resting his head against his teacher's shoulder and his feet were touching the leg of the child next to him.

Over the next hour of observation we saw the little boy touch, pat, poke, and pet a dozen children or more. None of the other children wished to be touched, but their negative reactions had no effect on his touching behavior. While he was not hyperactive, he seemed unable to stop breaking the rules of appropriate touching behavior.

◆

Tragically, many children like Brad are not aware of the source of their isolation. The frequent report card comment, "Must learn to keep hands to himself," is a reflection of the kind of behavior we are talking about. While most children can learn to control excessive touching by learning what is and what is not acceptable, dyssemic children such as Brad may benefit, at first, by being placed in situations where it is impossible to touch others at all.

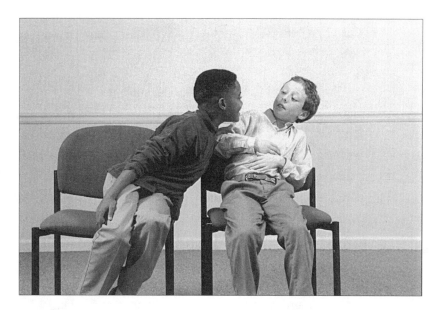

Fig. 2.7

The child on the left illustrates
an expressive touch dyssemia

■ TIPS FOR TEACHERS AND PARENTS ■
Helping Your Child Understand Touch

1. Through use of a touch silhouette, such as the one in figure 2.3, focus on the areas of the body that one may touch. Be sure to explain the different touch behaviors associated with various situations and people. For example, have your child indicate the places where it is OK to touch Mom versus a teacher, Mom at home versus Mom at church, etc.

☐

2. Touch the child in various places and ask him or her what is learned from this. Vary the places of touching (inside bodyline versus outside bodyline) and the intensity of the touch (for example, a pat versus a push).

☐

3. Observe others touching each other in natural settings and interactions (at school, the mall, church, at home). Discuss the ways in which touch communicates things between the people involved. Focus on what the child can learn about the internal states of others on the basis of their touching behavior. For example, based upon how a teacher is touching another child, should you or should you not do what that child has just done?

☐

4. Help your child to practice variation in his or her touching intensities and locations. Provide feedback regarding what the child is telling you through his or her touching.

☐

Even though we Americans prefer not to touch or be touched (or perhaps because of that), touch plays a significant role in our relationships. The teacher who knows how to rest a soft hand on the shoulder of a student who needs encouragement, the parent who gives a supportive hug to a child to encourage or reward a job well done, or the child who gives his or her teammate a properly intense "slap on the back" during a game are all "speaking" nonverbal language very effectively. On the other hand, those dyssemic children who misuse touch are likely to have interpersonal relationships that are fraught with tension, difficulty, and, ultimately, social rejection.

CHAPTER THREE:

RAISING HANDS: GESTURES AND POSTURES

RAISING HANDS:
GESTURES AND POSTURES

◇

In a fascinating book called *Manwatching,* Desmond Morris concluded that gestures and postures were often so culturally specific that ethnic background could be identified merely by looking at the way a person stood or used his or her hands. Indeed, the various nonverbal language *patterns of* specific cultures are most easily recognized through their respective gestures and postures. However, just as there are people who have verbal language deficits regardless of their specific native tongue, in any culture there also can be a nonverbal language dyssemia in the use of gestures and postures.

Even if we can speak a foreign language fluently, native speakers of that language have little difficulty identifying us, even at a distance, as foreigners. According to European researchers, some American postures are uniquely identifiable. We have attempted to show one of the most common American postures in figure 3.1. Our European colleagues called this the "John Wayne" posture. Further, we were told that Americans use their hands less and differently than other people. As Wallburga von Raffler-Engel has noted, in order to fully communicate in a foreign language, one must be *bikinesic* as well as bilingual. To be bikinesic is to be able to use the nonverbal as well as the verbal language of two cultures. Unfortunately, however, most Americans who

Fig. 3.1
The "John Wayne" posture

study foreign languages turn out to be bilingual and *monokinesic*. That is, they can speak two verbal languages but only their own nonverbal language. We may be speaking French, Italian, German, or Russian words, but our postures, gestures, tone of voice, and rhythm are still "saying" American! But what does this have to do with gestural and postural dyssemia? Although a child may speak English perfectly well, if he or she does not complement it with the appropriate gestures and postures, that child will have difficulty functioning effectively and therefore may not fit in even in his or her native land.

Gestures

From the simple learning of how to "wave bye-bye" to the more complex learning of intricate finger and hand positions which express an array of emotions, gestures play an exceedingly important role in our moment-to-moment interactions. Children who can both understand and send a broad repertoire of clear-meaning gestures may hold a distinct interpersonal advantage over those who cannot.

Most important gestures involve the hands, which convey a wide variety of effective information. Sometimes arms, hands, and fingers are used to produce "batons" which *emphasize, complement, or specify the meanings of words.* For example, when you want to communicate "Stop," a variety of gestures can accompany the word to achieve some different impacts. When someone is coming toward you, you may put your hand out. To cease commotion, you may wave your hand at waist level in front of your body. Figures 3.2, 3.3, and 3.4 demonstrate such gestures. If the word

"Stop" is accompanied by the hand motion in 3.2, the meaning is much stronger than it would be in the hand motion in 3.3. Of course, there is always the word "Stop" accompanied by the finger-pointing gesture in 3.4. This baton typically says, "I mean business," and frequently is used when teachers or parents are disciplining children.

Fig. 3.2
"Stop" is communicated through the straight arm and palm in front of the body

Fig. 3.3
"Cease commotion" is communicated by a wave at waist level

Fig. 3.4
The "I mean business" baton

While batons embellish words, other gestures can communicate information independently of words. Thus, in most areas of the world, the shake of the head usually means "no" and the nod of the head means "yes." Similarly, crossing the arms tightly in front of the chest most often indicates resistance to what is being communicated; sticking out the tongue communicates arrogance; tapping the foot generally communicates nervousness or impatience.

67

The Complexity of Gestural Communication

Since there are many blatant and subtle gestures that are used in daily interactions, it would be impossible and unproductive to try to list them all. However, we believe it is useful to be aware of *how much* there is to learn in order to master the complexities of gestural communication. This fact is not always easy to remember because *most of the time, gestures occur as background to the conversation and do not stand out.* At times, though, something happens to bring gestures to the forefront of our awareness, and then we can appreciate their communicative power.

We re-examined, without the sound, videotapes of children who had interpersonal adjustment problems. The effect, as hoped, was to magnify their gestural behaviors. It was clear that many of these children used their hands to communicate in rather stilted ways. Further, their gestures were not synchronized with one another or with their postures. In fact, their gestures were either difficult to follow or, if clear, were usually negative in tone. Julie was one such child we observed.

Gestures play an exceedingly important role in our moment-to-moment interactions. Children who can both understand and send a broad repertoire of clear-meaning gestures hold a distinct interpersonal advantage over those who cannot.

Twelve-year-old Julie was a very nice-looking pre-teen. Like many girls her age, she was beginning to experiment with makeup, talked incessantly about boys, clothes, and music, and was a fairly good student. However, other children, especially other girls, did not like her. While her parents and Julie were quite frustrated in their efforts to understand her peers, Julie's teachers were in a unique position to observe the situation. They told us that Julie talked to other children the way her teachers did, and the other children resented her for it. Julie's playground behavior proved the teachers were correct. Silent videotapes showed that Julie used adult gestures with her peers: she pointed her finger at them and waved it around in an authoritarian way; she folded her arms over her chest in an inappropriately adult fashion; she stared at them as if they were supposed to do her bidding. But the reality was that Julie was only another child like they were, not a teacher. Her behavior therefore resulted in her social rejection. *Helping Julie and her parents become aware of her gestural dyssemia led to a quick resolution of her problems.*

◆

Julie's expressive dyssemia provided us with a good demonstration of how important it is to know the variety of human gestures and further showed the importance of knowing when to use them appropriately. For example, had Julie and her friends been "playing" school, her use of teacher-type gestures would not have been so maladaptive. *Children need to know which gestures to use and when they are appropriate.*

Gestures add immensely to our ability both to send and to receive complete information about feelings. Further, in interpersonal relationships, gestures often provide the basis for the "true" meaning of a conversation. Therefore, gestural communication problems can also occur when a child's words and gestures do not match. Consider, for example, one child saying to another, "Get away from me!" If accompanied by a gesture meaning dislike, such as shown in figure 3.5, the message of rejection is clear. However, if the words "Let's go" were to accompany that gesture, the meaning would become vague; the words would be paired with a gesture of opposite meaning. Research shows that when verbal and nonverbal messages are discrepant, the nonverbal one

The more aware we are of how gestures affect our interpersonal interactions, the better the chance that our experiences will be positive.

69

Fig. 3.5
The "Get away from me" gesture

is more likely to be believed. This last point is crucial, especially when children are unaware of the gestures they use. Other people assume that our gestures match our internal states; therefore, what they see is what they respond to. Thus, we saw Julie being rejected for acting like a teacher on the outside, even though on the inside, she was just a lonely little girl.

The more aware we are of how gestures affect our interpersonal interactions, the better the chance that our experiences will be positive. Socially adept children are more likely to use appropriate gestures and be aware that they are using gestures effectively; in contrast, socially rejected children may have **expressive gestural dyssemia** that drives others away. These dyssemic children are usually unaware that their gestures are inappropriate.

■ **TIPS FOR TEACHERS AND PARENTS** ■
Helping Your Child Develop Better
Gestural Communication Skills

1. Make videotapes of your child in routine activities such as playing outside, sitting at work tables, waiting in line, having lunch, etc. Sit down with him or her and watch the tapes without the sound. (If you are trying to help a "troubled" child, do this with the child alone.) Observe and identify positive and negative gestures. Discuss the situational appropriateness of gestures. For example, was it right for that boy to wave when he left the room?

☐

2. Tape and watch TV shows or movies in which people often exaggerate gestures for effect. Discuss with the child the relationships between the characters involved. Demonstrate and discuss the relationship between gestures and the characters' emotional states and how one can use this information. For example, point out the gestures of one character, stop the tape, and talk about what is likely to happen next.

☐

3. Develop a cross-cultural program for studying gestures. Obtain magazines (such as *National Geographic, Stern,* or *Elle)* or TV shows from other countries, and identify differences in gestures and their meanings. See the "References" section for suggested readings; a good one is *Bodily Communication* by Michael Argyle.

☐

4. Set up "games" such as charades or other activities in which your child may only use gestures or other nonverbal patterns to communicate. Charades is an especially good training device that has sadly fallen out of use. It is a powerful nonverbal tool, however, and deserves resurrection. To play charades, prepare three types of cards: feeling cards (anger, boredom, etc.), method cards (space, facial expression, gestures, etc.), and send/receive cards. Spinners can also be prepared. Then have a child pick one card from the send/receive pile. When the card says "send," the child picks two other cards to determine which feeling and method are to be "sent." The child then acts out the feeling while the others try to guess what it is. When the child selects a "receive" card, another child picks the method and the feeling cards; the receiver then tries to guess the feeling.

☐

5. Watch mimes perform and discuss what they are "saying." (Never assume that all children understand these artists; it can be amazing how many children are simply lost when watching them.)

☐

6. Work with your child to generate a "dictionary" of gestures using self-made photographs, newspaper or magazine cut-outs, etc. Help him or her organize this dictionary and use it in specific nonverbal language tasks such as nonverbal charades (in much the same way as children use verbal-language dictionaries).

☐

Take a Stand: Posture

While gestures are associated with close-range conversations, body postures represent a form of nonverbal language that we can use to "read" others from afar as well as up close. As compared to gestures, *postures* involve most or all of one's body; they involve a combination of torso position, hand and arm location, foot location, head orientation, etc. Although there are many components to posture, we typically respond to each posture as a single unit of nonverbal behavior, a "message" that tells others about such things as our general mood, our degree of commitment to an activity, our basic attitudes, or our level of self-awareness.

> Postures involve most or all of one's body; they involve a combination of torso position, hand and arm location, foot location, head orientation, etc.

Teachers will tell you that they can often judge a class on the first day of school by looking around at the ways in which the students are sitting. Parents can often tell the kind of day their child will have by the way he or she sits at the breakfast table. While it is possible not to make any gestures or to avoid touching other people, *we cannot avoid showing a body posture that communicates something about our attitudes and feelings*. As a result, we are always communicating with others through our posture whether we want to or not. If children use postural communication effectively, they can improve their chances for social and academic success; if they don't, they may experience significant, unintentionally induced problems.

To demonstrate the power of posture, examine the series of photos in figure 3.6a–f. To make a point, we have varied only the position of the child's hands and arms. Note the different perceptions you have of this person as you move through the series of photos. The same boy may be seen as anything from a strong, ready-to-go kind of individual to a total "nerd"—primarily be-

Fig. 3.6. THE POWER OF POSTURE

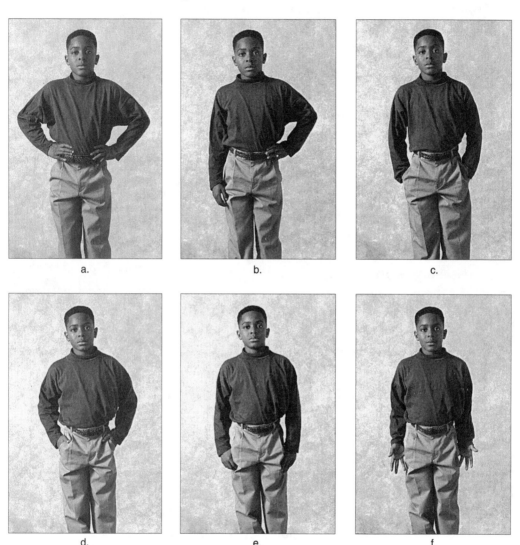

a. b. c.

d. e. f.

cause of his body posture. One can only guess the social impact of these postural differences in a school setting. Such nuances of body posture played a significant role in the difficulties of a high school student named Margaret.

An extremely bright and capable student, Margaret earned extra money by working as a temporary office worker after school and on Saturdays. Her job involved being sent out to different businesses and working in their offices. Success was determined not only by the quality of her work but also by whether or not the clients asked her to come back. Margaret was rarely asked to return. Candid discussion between Margaret's supervisor and a few of her employers revealed that part of her problem was the way she seemed to slouch in her chair while working, a posture that gave these employers the impression that she was disinterested and not very capable. It should be noted that Margaret was anything but disinterested, but her posture said otherwise.

◆

Upon consultation with Margaret and her teachers, we determined that a significant source of her difficulties, at work and in school, originated in what we have come to call her "resting posture." A **resting posture** is the posture we assume when we are essentially feeling neutral. In that we cannot avoid a posture, then, the resting posture is probably the one that is most often seen by others. Margaret slouched badly; when seated, she leaned forward with her back bent and her head down. Her shoulders were rounded forward, making her look much older than she was. Her employers were correct; she looked disinterested and incapable. In essence, Margaret had an **expressive posture dyssemia**; she was not sending out an accurate indication of her feelings through her postures. Making her aware of her postural dyssemia and its possible negative consequences with her employers, teachers, and peers (coupled with some old-fashioned lessons in walking, sitting, and standing) seemed to help improve the impressions of her employers.

"Resting" postures are not the only body positions that communicate relationship information. Let's consider the average school classroom, a place where body postures play a very important role. Imagine a good teacher at work; he or she uses body postures expressively in a very effective manner. One teacher we knew learned to use her desk for different postural positions depending upon the importance of the lesson at hand. If the topic were a loose and lively one, she would stand, legs crossed, leaning back on the front of her desk. For a more serious topic, she would stand firmly on her two feet at the side of her desk. For the most serious topic she would stand behind her desk leaning forward, with her hands resting on the desk top. Most of the children whose receptive postural language ability was adequate would respond appropriately according to her changes in posture. However, in several of her classes, she noticed a few children who did not seem to alter their behaviors in response to her postures. These children, it turns out, were either not aware that she was assuming different positions or, if they were aware, they did not realize that these different postural positions had any specific meanings. These students may have had a **receptive posture dyssemia.**

It is sometimes hard to believe that certain people cannot understand the meanings of various postures. We have found that a good way to identify children with receptive postural dyssemia is to use old silent movies as well as videotapes without sound (described earlier in our discussion of gestures). Videotapes of soap operas are also particularly useful. Watching these rather melodramatic shows without sound makes it easier to focus on a wide variety of postures in adults and children who are interacting under a variety of emotional conditions. People who cannot follow what's going on without hearing the spoken words suffer from a distinct interpersonal disadvantage.

> W e cannot avoid showing a body posture that communicates something about our attitudes and feelings.

Walking

Up to this point we have talked about relatively static postures—that is, postures that are used by people when they are
basically still. However, when people move themselves from
place to place, they also engage in a sequence of postural changes
which can communicate information. What we are describing is
a "gait" or, more plainly, a way of walking. Impressionists sometimes make walking a primary way of copying a celebrity's
personality. From actors like John Wayne to rock stars like Mick
Jagger, a person's walk can be as identifiable as a signature.

In our everyday lives, we recognize the information that
walking can transmit, from the shaky gait of the elderly person to
the threatening swagger of the "tough guy" lumbering down a
street. We form our initial "long distance" impressions of others
based upon their walking style. Consider how people viewed Jill:

Jill was a fourth grade student in a small public school. An
intelligent and friendly girl, she was basically unhappy and
according to her parents, she seemed to attract some pretty
rough kids as friends. While Jill and her parents were at a loss
in trying to understand her inability to make the friends that
they would have preferred, her teacher recognized the problem; it was the way Jill "carried herself." Specifically, her
teacher believed that Jill walked in a very masculine manner,
a manner that said to other people, "I am a tough, hard,
nonfeminine person who does not want to be around anybody
who is not like me." The unfortunate thing was that Jill felt, and
is, in fact, very feminine, and as a person she was very unlike
the impression that her gait communicated. With some well-
placed discussions and some practice, Jill was able to remediate her form of dyssemia, alter her style of movement, and
express what she truly felt. Then she formed relationships
with peers who were more compatible with her sense of who
she really was.

◆

Gaits not only affect our relationships, but also how we adjust to unfamiliar settings. Examine what happened to one young woman, who was raised in the South, when she went to New York City.

Claire was offered a summer internship at a major publishing firm in New York City. She gladly accepted, and in early June, she moved to New York. On her first day, she was extremely nervous not only about the job, but also about being on the streets of the city. When she arrived at her office, several seasoned veterans of New York gave her some much-needed lessons in posture and gait. They told her that she should walk in a manner which told others that she was not a tourist and that she could take care of herself. Claire was advised to walk rapidly and not to window shop; she was to keep her eyes down and not make eye contact with other people. Further, she was told to carry her "good shoes" in a bag or back pack and to wear tennis or running shoes; she was also told not to wear any dangling earrings. After a few days, she was looking like a New Yorker. Claire was certainly not a native, but her nonverbal language said she was to all those who were reading her behavior.

◆

One can generalize from the New York City experience described above. Most of the time, others believe we are the way we present ourselves nonverbally. If we stand and move with confidence, others perceive us as strong and competent; if we carry ourselves with confidence, we are more likely to succeed.

■ **TIPS FOR PARENTS AND TEACHERS** ■
Helping Your Child Develop Better Postural Communication

1. Have the child observe others in natural settings. Identify and discuss the meanings of various postures. Focus on whether he or she should approach or avoid people with various postures.

☐

2. Make videotapes of your child in various activities, and watch the tapes without sound. Focus on his or her postures and discuss their meanings.

☐

3. Make a "dictionary" of postures using magazine pictures or "home-made" photos. Label the postures according to meaning; for example, "tired," "bored," "angry," etc.

☐

4. Play "feeling" charades as described in the tips on gestures, using postures as the prime method of nonverbal communication. Be sure your child has a chance both to give clues (expressive communication) and receive them (receptive communication).

☐

5. Provide practice in "long distance" communication. Have the child describe, purely on the basis of posture, the internal feelings, attitudes, and characteristics being communicated by various people he or she is observing.

☐

We've discussed the nonverbal channels of gestures and postures. Both are important in effective social interaction, and expressive or receptive dyssemias in either can be a source of social rejection. However, both forms of communication can be learned or remediated through the *directed* efforts of parents and teachers.

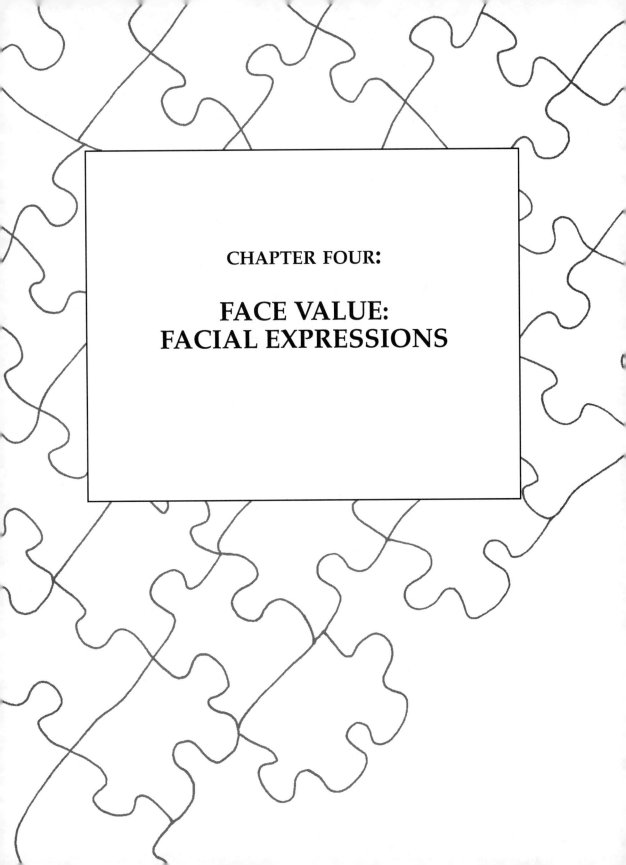

CHAPTER FOUR:

FACE VALUE:
FACIAL EXPRESSIONS

FACE VALUE:
FACIAL EXPRESSIONS

◇

Most of the time, we are only vaguely aware of one another's rhythms, time usage, postures, gestures, and personal space. It usually takes a strikingly positive or negative event in one of these channels to catch our attention. However, faces always catch our attention. In fact, in any meeting, people spend more time looking at one another's faces—especially the eyes—than anywhere else. Doing so affords us valuable clues about one another's feelings and attitudes. In addition to the eyes, other parts of the face also have the ability to communicate feelings. We speak of that ability in phrases such as "his face dropped" or "you should have seen the look on his face" or "she looked down her nose at me" or "he was down in the mouth."

Given that the ability to send and receive facial information accurately is so central, slight problems in processing this information can cause significant interpersonal difficulties. Even something so basic as the "resting face" can cause problems. Parallel to the "resting posture," which we discussed earlier, the **"resting face"** is the expression we have on when we are essentially in "neutral." Since other people do not know what is going on inside us, they will interpret our facial expression as it appears to them, not as it feels to us. Thus, although we may be feeling little or nothing, our "resting face" may be communicating something positive or negative. In the case of a young high school student, Mary, it was something negative.

Mary was fourteen and dyssemic; she had trouble expressing facial information. Mary said that she'd had trouble making friends since she began junior high school. Her attempts to talk to others had generally been rebuffed. The teachers at her school were always struck by her facial expression. Mary's mouth was tightly pursed and her nose was scrunched up as if she were smelling and tasting something awful. Her "resting face" contributed significantly to Mary's problems in starting relationships, and *she was completely unaware of how her "resting face" looked.* Mary was actually a bright, very nice young girl who wanted to belong and be liked, but her resting face was giving the opposite message. As the result of a private conversation with a teacher whom she trusted, Mary was given a simple "homework" assignment designed to make her more aware of her facial expressions by practicing in front of a mirror. After a few weeks of practice, a more positive resting face paid off for Mary. She reported improvements in her relationships with peers. Further, consistent with the fact that nonverbal communication takes place out of our awareness, others said that "there was something different about Mary," but they did not know what. And she never told them.

◆

Facing Problems: Receptive and Expressive Facial Dyssemia

As with the other types of nonverbal language, there are both expressive and receptive processes in facial communication. In almost every interaction, people exchange a steady stream of information about their attitudes and feelings through their facial expressions. Effective human interaction depends upon our abilities to accurately "send" our feelings and attitudes and to accurately "read" those of others. Social difficulties are often related to problems with making eye contact.

Effective eye contact and the appropriate use of smiling are the two most frequently noted characteristics of socially successful children. Eye contact is necessary for the exchange of all visual, nonverbal information. Studies of interactions have shown that we look at the people we're communicating with more when we're listening to them than when we're speaking. During a conversation, we spend about 30 to 60 percent of the time looking at the other person's face. If we don't look at others this much while we're interacting with them, we lose valuable interpersonal information. Stanford, a thirteen-year-old boy with expressive facial dyssemia, found out how poor eye contact can hinder peer relationships.

Stanford seemed like a child who was always lost in a fog. He did not seem to know when he was supposed to speak in a conversation, he couldn't play games properly, and he had a knack for saying the wrong thing at the wrong time. Stanford was "out of sync" with his classmates; he was avoided by others and had few if any friends. After we observed Stanford throughout the day, it became obvious that he simply did not look at others. When speaking, he averted his gaze either to the side or downward. Others never knew whether or not Stanford was "receiving" their messages because he gave no properly timed visual cues. Further, when he spoke, others had difficulty determining when he was finished because he did not use the normal eye movements associated with the conclusion of a statement (the so-called "it's your turn" glance). Once Stanford became aware of his eye contact dyssemia, he was a willing partner in a program to help rectify this deficiency and improve his interpersonal interactions.

◆

Even with adequate eye contact, it is still possible to have difficulty reading facial expressions accurately. The majority of children can differentiate among the varying faces presented in figures 4.1–4.4. While the most easily identified emotion is "happiness," our research has shown that sadness, anger, and fear are more difficult to "read." For example, a child with **receptive facial dyssemia** may misread a sad face as an angry one and thus respond with avoidance or anger instead of closeness and caring.

FACIAL EXPRESSIONS COMMUNICATE EMOTIONS

Fig. 4.1
Anger

Fig. 4.2
Fear

Fig. 4.3
Happiness

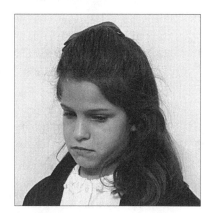

Fig. 4.4
Sadness

In other instances, facial expressions may be missed entirely. These errors can increase the likelihood of relationship problems in children. For example, one teacher told us of a boy who was unable to accurately "read" the stern face used by many teachers (and parents) to command a child's attention. When the teacher gave the stern expression to this youngster, he just kept on with what he was doing. On one or two occasions he looked up at her and asked, "Why are you standing there?" She became very angry with him until she realized that he really could not "read" the facial information she was sending.

Reading faces accurately is only half the story. We must also be able to produce facial expressions that reveal our true feelings. We once studied a group of children who had significant relationship problems. We suspected that nonverbal communication skills, especially involving facial expressions, were involved. To test this possibility, we asked them to make facial expressions which reflect various feelings, and then we photographed them. We were surprised to find that, for several children, all the photographs looked essentially the same. The children in our study were unaware of it, but they were using *similar facial expressions* to communicate *different emotions*—actions sure to increase their chances of being misinterpreted and failing interpersonally. Interpersonal problems can develop when a child unknowingly uses the wrong facial expression or the correct facial expression with the wrong *intensity* (for example, laughing when smiling is appropriate or crying when a slightly sad expression is called for). The impact of this type of communication error is shown by "Mr. Doom."

Wayne was a practice teacher who was having some trouble relating to his students during class. When he was lecturing about technical topics, he was fine. However, when he attempted to have informal conversations with students or other teachers, his inability to produce the appropriate facial expressions became a problem. It seemed that Wayne was only able to produce sullen or serious faces during informal conversations. His students were aware of his tendency toward serious expressions and jokingly called him "Mr. Doom." Over time, the incongruence between Wayne's words, which were often playful, and his somber facial expressions began to cause problems as his students became increasingly uncomfortable with him.

Wayne was advised by his supervisor to try to smile more when he was talking with his students; however, this did not solve the problem. It turned out that Wayne also had a problem in what is called *modulation.* That is, he was unable to smile in moderation. If he tried to smile, he had to laugh out loud. Consequently, some of his students saw him as foolish, and his authority and credibility as a teacher suffered.

◆

It has been our experience that, like Wayne, some dyssemic people have trouble modulating the type and intensity of emotion expressed through the face. While potentially creating problems for adults, such inabilities are especially damaging to some children. Regardless of their good intentions, the fact that these youngsters are unable to produce the correct type and intensity of facial expressions can create interpersonal situations characterized by confusion and anxiety. Many times, awareness and practice are all that may be needed to correct this **expressive facial dyssemia.**

Social Success and Facial Expressiveness
While the exact number of dyssemic children with facial expression deficits is unknown, a study we completed on over a thousand children between the ages of six and ten suggests that

there are more than just a few. We assessed the ability to both read and send emotions accurately via facial expressions. We found that between seven and ten percent of these children had significant difficulty in either reading or producing specific emotional expressions. Further, these dyssemic children were more prone to be disliked and isolated from their peers; they were also more likely to be unhappy as compared to the children who properly processed facial information.

Besides showing how prevalent facial expression dyssemia may be, the results of our study also indicated that children who were above average in processing facial information tended to be better adjusted. In our study of what differentiated socially successful from socially rejected children, we found that facial expression abilities were mentioned time and time again. Socially successful children were more frequently said to "have a bright look" on their faces, to "smile almost all the time," to "look happy and satisfied," to have "eyes that were alive," and the like. Such characteristics certainly played a part in Laura's social success.

F*acial processing dyssemias may represent an identifiable and correctable source for many interpersonal difficulties.*

Everyone in the high school knew Laura. She was president of the student government association, president of her class, and a member of many other clubs. She was the sort of girl who could do everything, but in fact, she actually did very little. Laura had a simple philosophy and belief about herself which she stated openly. "I can encourage other people to do their best, and I never take credit for anything, myself. I always put the credit with the people who do things. Somehow, I can get people to reach beyond their own limits." People who knew her agreed. Laura's greatest skill was being the most "personable girl in the school." Her resting face and smile made people feel at ease; her facial expression communicated interest in others and what they had to say. Other students loved being around her and seeing the look on her face when they did something special. Laura believed that she was a catalyst, "a chemical that makes other chemicals work better." She was indeed, but her magic lay not in a true chemical reaction, but in the reactions others had to her. Laura's nonverbal communication skills significantly contributed to her election as the most outstanding member of her graduating class—most impressive for a girl who described herself as being able to do so "very little."

◆

■ **TIPS FOR PARENTS AND TEACHERS** ■
Helping Your Child Develop Better Skills
in Communicating through Facial Expressions

1. Develop a "dictionary" of facial expressions, pasting pictures of various expressions on the pages and having your child label each expression.

□

2. Develop a set of facial expression stimuli by cutting out pictures from magazines. Using these like facial "flash cards," ask the child to give rapid responses, saying what the expression on the card is. Or, ask the child to act out a response to that expression, indicating good understanding of the face.

□

3. Teach the child how to practice facial expressions (especially resting faces) by using a mirror. Have him or her practice major facial expressions (fear, anger, sadness, and happiness) for at least five minutes per day.

□

4. Use an instant or video camera, ask your child to demonstrate a particular expression, and then photograph it. Examine the photos with the child, and discuss the accuracy of his or her expressions. For example, does the child's idea of a sad expression really look sad to the child? Does it look sad to him? Focus on the way the child's facial muscles feel when producing various expressions.

□

5. Play "face charades" in which only facial expressions may be used to provide clues to various emotional states or attitudes listed on some cards drawn by the child. Have the child both "send" and "receive."

☐

6. Describe various situations which a child might encounter, and require him or her to communicate using only the face. For example, "Imagine that you are at the supermarket and need help finding a particular item. What facial expression should you use when asking for guidance?" "What sort of facial expression on others would indicate that they might be helpful to you?"

☐

7. Watch soap operas or movies with the sound turned off. Focus on the facial expressions of the characters, and attempt to follow the plot. Stop the tape at random, and ask the child to describe what is likely to happen next.

☐

8. In public settings, such as shopping centers or athletic events, observe people's faces from a distance and try to guess the nature of their conversations and relationships. This can be turned into a game in which the child gets points for perceptions that agree with those of the tutor.

☐

9. Do "cross-channel" exercises. For example, show your child a picture of a very sad face, then ask the how the person depicted would say the following sentence: "I'm going into my room now, but I'll be back later." Similarly, given the sad face, ask the child to portray the most likely posture of the person depicted. (Note: Cross-channeling can be done as part of teaching exercises for all of the forms of nonverbal language described in this book.)

☐

Nonverbal facial expression information is central to our daily lives. For those able to read and produce these types of interpersonal cues, facial expressions provide an avenue to successful interactions and relationships. Facial expression processing dyssemias, however, may represent an identifiable and correctable source for many interpersonal difficulties.

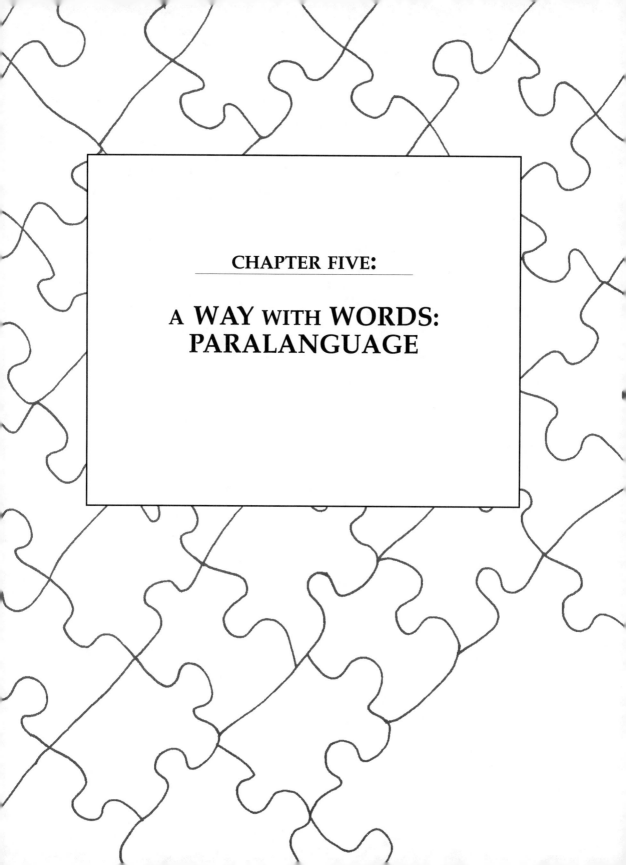

CHAPTER FIVE:

A WAY WITH WORDS: PARALANGUAGE

A WAY WITH WORDS: PARALANGUAGE

◇

So far, we have emphasized the impact of nonverbal information that can be *seen*. Now we turn to the forms of nonverbal communication that can be *heard*. How people sound when they speak is a very important indicator of how they feel. We've all probably had someone tell us they felt fine in such a way as to express that in fact something was wrong. In such instances, if we were nonverbally astute, we responded to the way the person sounded as opposed to the words that he or she may have used. This ability to pick up the feelings behind the words is an important social skill that is crucial to the development and maintenance of relationships. An important, parallel social skill is the ability to accurately express how we feel by the use of appropriate sounds. These skills are important because it has been found that nearly one-third of the emotional meaning invested in conversations is carried by what is called *paralanguage.*

Paralanguage refers to all the aspects of sound which accompany words or act independently of them to communicate emotion. Included here are such things as tone, loudness, intensity of voice, and the sounds such as humming and whistling which are uttered between or instead of words. Often the importance of paralanguage is obscured when we have access to visual nonverbal information like facial expressions, postures, gestures, and so on. However, much like turning down the sound on a television to accentuate the visual signals, talking on the telephone enhances our dependence on paralinguistics. This fact makes some people uncomfortable on the phone, especially those of us who are not adept at this kind of nonverbal communication.

We are going to describe four aspects of paralanguage that are important to the communication of our feelings: nonverbal sound patterns, speed of talking, intensity of speech, and different tones of voice. The inability to master these cues and clues of paralanguage leaves a child more vulnerable to interpersonal failure.

Very young children use a number of sounds and noises to communicate their needs and desires to adults. Such vocalizations aren't used as often by older children, but they occur frequently enough in conversations to make life difficult for a child who cannot express or understand the meaning of sound patterns.

Using the nonword "mmmmmmm" clearly indicates liking of something, while a hissing sound indicates a clear dislike. In addition to communicating such likes and dislikes, parents and teachers have often used nonword vocalizations to guide the behavior of children. This assumes, however, that children understand the meaning of these sounds. An example of this is a child who was seen on a school playground.

Paralanguage refers to all aspects of sound used to communicate emotion. Included are the tone, loudness, intensity of voice, and sounds such as humming and whistling which accompany words or act independently of them.

Several children were playing near the fence of the playground; there was an open gate near them which led to the street. Four children broke off from the main group and walked toward the gate as if they were going to go through it. A teacher was standing near the gate, reading, and noticed the children's approach out of the corner of her eye. Without looking up she uttered, "mmmm—mmmmmm—mmmmmmmm," with each "mmm" being higher in pitch than the last and with the last being said in a sort of sing-song tone. (We hope you know what we are describing; to most of us it means, "You'd better stop and think about what you're going to do!") As a tribute to the power of such sounds, three of the four children stopped dead in their tracks; however, the fourth child kept right on going and the teacher had to run after her. In this case, the child did not respond because she had a **receptive nonverbal vocalization deficit.** If the teacher had been unaware of this child's dyssemia, she might have assumed that the child was defiant and responded accordingly.

◆

Nonverbal vocalizations can clearly be quite powerful when children know how to interpret them. However, these sounds can have a similarly large impact if a child has an **expressive problem** with their use. Often a relatively small thing such as the constant clearing of one's throat or an abrasive or high-pitched laugh can contribute to a child's social rejection. Such was the case with Marla, a friendly but socially unsuccessful child and adult.

In high school, it seemed that everyone knew why people stayed away from Marla, but no one, not even her parents, told her. Marla's laugh was so shrill and abrasive that people could not help but notice it. In class, when she laughed about something, her peers would shudder. Her teacher, sensitive to the problem, found himself trying not to say humorous things in order to reduce the frequency of the laughter. People who were with Marla when she laughed were often embarrassed. She rarely went out on a second date. This was a girl who was sweet and kind to others, and certainly did not desire or deserve the level of scorn and avoidance her laugh produced. Marla did not understand why she had so little luck with friends, especially males. She developed the belief that there were "no boys that she could go out with at her high school." When she grew up, she lived in several major cities, dating and trying to meet people. In each town, the result was the same; she found herself alone and then relocated because "there were no men in those places." Through a very sensitive letter, a former friend and co-worker told Marla about her laugh and its effects. Hurt and angry, Marla rejected the friend's suggestion about the source of her problems. Today, at the age of forty-five, Marla is still socially isolated and living alone. Her laugh is still quite abrasive.

◆

Parents and teachers are often much more aware than children of the sorts of problems associated with dyssemias such as Marla's. Not always successful but nevertheless necessary are sensitive, well-placed suggestions regarding the problem pattern. When given in private by someone whom the child trusts, such suggestions can have dramatic effects on the interpersonal and emotional worlds of youngsters.

Fast Talk: Rate and Synchronicity of Speech

Many of us have seen the TV commercials in which an actor talks incredibly fast; sometimes the actor portrays a harried business man, at other times a super-efficient employee. The producers of these commercials know that beyond the words used, the actor's rate of speech is communicating something more to the listeners. The same is true in everyday life. In an academic setting, a teacher who speaks rapidly may be perceived as being very well prepared and knowledgeable. In other contexts, rapid speech can have an irritating or intimidating effect on others. Slow talking also affects others. From a student giving a report, slow speech may seem to signify insecurity or a lack of preparation; conversely, a parent's slow talking can have a soothing effect on a distraught child.

Ideally, we should be able to modulate our rate of speech according to the situation we are in, and it is also important to synchronize our rate of speech with that of others. Most of us have a preferred rate of speech, but we should be flexible enough to speed up or slow down depending on whom we are talking with.

As with other types of nonverbal language, most people are not aware of their own rate of speech or the impression their rate of speech can make on others. Bob and Ray, a delightful comedy team who began in old-time radio, have a classic skit which makes this point nicely. In it, Ray has only a few minutes to interview Bob, who is a member of STOA—"Slow Talkers of America." The skit shows Ray's increasing tension as he waits for each and every word that comes in an agonizingly slow manner from Bob.

Much of the comedy in the skit arises from Bob's **expressive speech rate dyssemia**—his inability to speed up his speech to accommodate Ray. Bob also exhibits a **receptive speech rate deficit**—he does not know how to read the proper cues indicating whose turn it is to talk. People like Bob will continue to talk in a slow monotone that allows no input from the other person; these are also the kinds of people who are likely to interrupt others in the middle of a thought. In essence they cannot get "in sync," and as a result, their interactions tend to become more and more strained.

Synchronicity of rate of speech is important for positive conversations. At the very least, if synchronicity cannot be obtained, then we should be sensitive to our differences as individuals.

Synchronicity of rate of speech is important for positive conversations. At the very least, if synchronicity cannot be obtained, then we should be sensitive to our differences as individuals.

Choosing Words Carefully: Emphasis and Variation in Speech

Consider the following sentence: "Mary's lending me her book." These five words, when written out as they are here, present a potentially confusing message if one is forced to interpret them without the benefit of cues such as word emphasis, tonal variation, and speech volume. To demonstrate our point, please read the sentence five times, each time emphasizing a different word. We have described below what changing the word emphasis does to the meaning of the sentence.

> 1. **Mary's** lending me her book.
>   (Not anyone else is)
> 2. Mary's **lending** me her book.
>   (Not giving it, just lending)
> 3. Mary's lending **me** her book.
>   (No one else, just me)
> 4. Mary's lending me **her** book.
>   (It belongs to Mary)
> 5. Mary's lending me her **book.**
>   (Not anything else)

Awareness of word emphasis is crucial to effective communication. If a child is not able to accurately interpret the different emphases in the words of teachers or peers, he or she is at a distinct disadvantage because of a **receptive dyssemia** in this area. Further, if a child cannot vary his or her own speech emphases appropriately, miscommunication is a likely result because of the child's **expressive dyssemia.**

In addition to word emphasis, as shown in the above example, variations in volume can enhance what we are trying to say. Without such fluctuations, speakers talk in a monotone. *Individuals who speak in a monotone can be perceived as dull and unattractive and stand an increased chance of being socially rejected.*

Speaking Up: Tone of Voice

There are times that the importance of what we say is outweighed by how we say it. The tone of voice allows us, paradoxically, to say "I hate you," and communicate "I love you," and vice versa. *In the subtlety of voice tone, we find what may be the most important aspect of nonverbal language.* It should come as no surprise that among the most destructive nonverbal language dyssemias are those involving an inability to accurately read or express meaning through tone of voice.

Tone of voice is something we respond to long before we react to the actual meanings of words. Consider how "Baby Richie" responded:

The proud parents of a "brilliant" six-month-old child, Richie, came to visit us. They were very excited about little Richie's intellectual abilities and liked to show him off. The major measure of his "genius" was that even at his early age, Richie could understand the *meanings* of words. To prove this, his father looked at him, and with a big grin and wide-open eyes, asked, "How big is Richie?" Richie always responded to the question with a "so big" sign with his hands and arms. His parents were so pleased with their brilliant son.

However, what they had failed to realize was that the words, "How big is Richie" were always said in a specific, rhythmic sing-song way, and in a particular tone of voice. We speculated that it was these cues Richie was responding to and not the words. To test this idea, we approached him and with the same emphasis and tone of voice said "Pizza pie and ice cream." Richie responded with his now classic "so big" gesture.

◆

Because responsiveness to tone of voice is so basic, it seems to take precedence over verbal communication whenever the two are discrepant with one another. For instance, to use the example cited earlier, if a speaker says, "I hate you" in a loving tone of voice, the listener will respond to the tone rather than the words and will feel loved rather than hated.

For another example of verbal-nonverbal discrepancy, recall the case in which the teacher invited questions from her students in such a way as to actually discourage them from asking questions. Remember that at the end of her lecture, the teacher stated, "If anyone has any questions about anything that I have said, please ask. I want to answer all of your questions," but not one student raised his or her hand, even those who had seemed eager to ask questions only a few moments earlier. The reason for this was a discrepancy between the teacher's verbal and nonverbal messages to the students. First, the tone of voice used by the teacher was insincere; second, her rate of speech became very rapid as she completed her presentation, as if she were trying to get finished quickly and go elsewhere; finally, she glanced at her watch. The result? No one asked any questions. While her words said "Ask questions," no one did because her nonverbal behaviors said not to.

> *In the subtlety of voice tone, we find what may be the most important aspect of nonverbal language.*

Tone of voice is often beyond our awareness. This is not a problem for most people who have learned pleasing and socially effective ways of speaking, but for those whose voice tones are abrasive and contribute to their social difficulties, it is a different matter. Comedians have emphasized such abrasive qualities. For example, the comedy show "Saturday Night Live" presented the 'Whiners' and the 'Loud Family.' The 'Whiners' sounded as though they were complaining about everything, and the 'Loud Family' shouted their conversations. True to the nonverbal code, the 'Whiners' and the 'Loud Family' were not aware that they were breaking any paralinguistic rules. However, the reactions of the other characters as well as those of the audience demonstrated the aversive qualities of their voice patterns.

Tone of voice is a prime communicator of emotion. To know the emotional state of others with whom we are interacting is to be in touch with them at the most complete and basic level; to be unaware of their feelings is to invite confusion and turmoil into interpersonal relationships. Herein lies the importance of understanding others through their tones of voice. Consider what happened to Ben:

Ben was a fourth-grader whose teacher was exasperated with him. She said that Ben would not respond to her requests to stop what he was doing and move on to the next task. Observing the classroom led to an understanding of this problem. Like many good teachers, Ben's was capable of using her voice tones very effectively; often just a slight variation in her tone resulted in an expected and clear response from her class. Ben was the exception. During our observation, the teacher asked the class to quiet down and all of them did—except Ben. The teacher reiterated, "Ben, be quiet please," but Ben kept talking. Then, with a sharp edge in her voice she said simply, "BEN!" He stopped and looked up at her and said, "Are you angry with me?" Here was a clear example of a **receptive voice tone dyssemia.**

◆

In perhaps the most difficult speech of his presidency, Ronald Reagan spoke to the nation following the explosion of the space shuttle Challenger. In what could only be described as a masterful use of tone of voice, Mr. Reagan spoke with a softness and a gentleness that seemed to evoke, in most people, a memory of a calming, in-control parent telling us that everything was going to be all right. Through his tone of voice and other nonverbal language, he allayed the nation's fears and helped us to move forward from the tragedy. For a more common example of **expressive voice tone ability,** consider the teacher we observed in a class of fourth graders. This young woman was incredibly skilled in using her tone of voice to guide and control her classroom. When students were busily working, all of her comments were said in a gentle and upbeat manner; when someone began to act up a bit, one could trace a parallel shift in her voice tone designed to "correct" the course of the lesson. All good teachers can do this; conversely, many teachers who have trouble managing their classrooms cannot.

■ TIPS FOR PARENTS AND TEACHERS ■
Helping Your Child to Decipher Paralanguage

1. Using videotapes of soap operas or movies, have your child turn his or her back to the screen. Ask the child to then use paralinguistic cues to describe the facial expressions, postures, and gestures of the actors.

☐

2. Using a tape recorder, develop an "audio dictionary" of voice tones that reflect various emotions and attitudes.

☐

3. Have the child practice the same sentence or word while communicating different things. An example is the word "Okay." Ask your child to say this word with proper intonation in response to a number of varying statements. For instance, "Go to your room" (said angrily); "We're going to the amusement park!"; "We need to wait thirty minutes before we leave for the store"; etc. Help your child to monitor the ways in which his or her voice tone changes the meaning of words and sentences.

☐

4. Say the same sentence several times to the child, each time varying your tone. Ask the child to describe what he or she is "reading" and to describe appropriate or inappropriate reactions to you.

☐

5. Play "paralanguage charades" in which emotional or personality characteristics such as friendliness, grumpiness, sadness, trustworthiness and such are communicated through sounds only (no actual words). Have the child both "send" as well as "receive" clues.

☐

6. Develop games in which your child exercises his or her voice tones in such a way as to gain control over them. For example, as the child is telling you a story or reading a paragraph, call out an emotion (sad, happy, angry, etc.) and require the child to shift to that voice tone without stopping the reading or talking. Conversely, read a passage and ask the child to call out your emotional state as you suddenly change your tone of voice.

☐

7. Have a child listen to his or her laugh and modulate it for different circumstances.

☐

8. Have your child practice speaking loudly versus softly, rapidly versus slowly, and so on. Have the child control these variables as you call out instructions. For example, start out by saying "soft and slow," then change to "loud and slow," etc. Audiotape the child's performance and listen to the tapes with him or her.

☐

9. Do "cross-channeling" between paralanguage and other nonverbal parts of speech. Have the child "receive" a message given paralinguistically and respond appropriately along another channel, such as through gestures or facial expressions. Or use a gesture with a child and ask that he or she respond to it paralinguisitically.

☐

The flow of words is accompanied by an even greater stream of paralanguage cues that can change the meaning of interpersonal situations without warning. The fact that nearly 40 percent of interpersonal information is communicated through the sorts of things we have discussed in this chapter should indicate just how important expressive and receptive deficits in this area can be. While it may be possible for a dyssemic child to get along with others to some degree if he or she has a problem in time usage, a disability in the use of paralanguage is more serious and may require intensive remedial efforts such as those we will describe in Part Two.

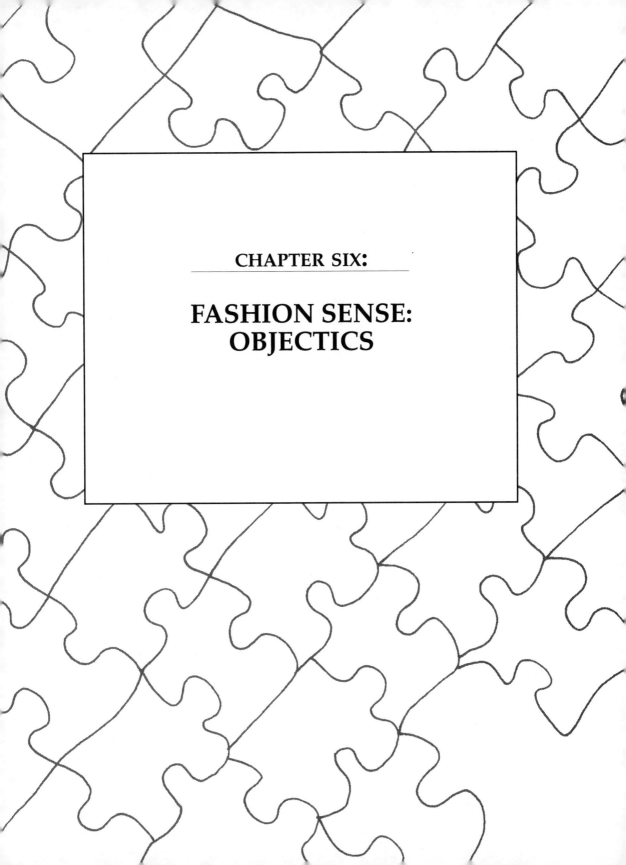

CHAPTER SIX:

FASHION SENSE: OBJECTICS

FASHION SENSE: OBJECTICS

◇

We've been discussing nonverbal behavior patterns dealing with the location, position, and movement of the body, as well as the use of voice. For the most part, people are unaware of these channels of communication and do not try to control them. In this chapter, we will turn to a slightly different channel of nonverbal language called **objectics;** it deals with things that many of us can control—*our style of dress and other ways in which we communicate to others through our appearance.* Objectic signals include such things as cosmetics, clothing, jewelry, hairstyles, perfumes, and deodorants.

In contrast to other nonverbal communication, objectic communications are characterized by one crucially important difference. *Our fashions, hairstyles, and such reflect a rapidly changing aspect of our culture.* Whereas a particular gesture or facial expression may remain the same from generation to generation, what is "in" and what is "out" can change at any moment. Proper communication through appearance can only be maintained if you are in tune with your culture's changing sense of fashion. This factor makes objectics a very complex area of nonverbal language, both expressively and receptively.

> O *bjectic signals are controllable; they include our style of dress and other ways in which we communicate to others through our appearance.*

◇

Style of Dress

Something magical seems to happen to youngsters between the ages of eleven and thirteen. One morning they awaken their parents earlier than usual because they are in the bathroom showering, blow-drying their hair, applying coverups, and splashing on aftershave or perfume. This sudden awareness of appearance is usually a reliable marker of adolescence.

Style of dress communicates that individuals are part of a group, and it helps them to avoid standing out as strange or different. For example, *young* adolescents tend to follow somewhat rigid rules of fashion. Remember that the particular jeans your teenager "must have" may be just as important for school as your fashionable outfit may be for the office. The message for each respective group is, "I am a safe, predictable person to be around"; "I am like you"; "You can trust me."

Style of dress is unique in nonverbal language because there have been attempts to write down its rules. We are referring to dress codes for schools and social settings such as restaurants. One of the more successful attempts to tell people how to dress was developed by John Malloy, whose books for aspiring business professionals on how to "dress for success" became bestsellers. Just walk down Park Avenue in New York at noon, and you'll see that many of his rules for business dressing are being followed to the present day.

If it truthfully reflects inner feelings and attitudes, then a person's style can be an effective way of attracting potential new friends. However, if style does not reflect one's true nature, troubles such as Nan experienced may be the result.

Sixteen-year-old Nan's major complaint was that she was a "creep magnet." She said that no matter where she went, she always seemed to attract boys who were, as she termed them, "creeps." The creeps only liked her physical appearance and did not care about anything beyond that. Clearly, Nan's style of dress was her problem; she wore makeup and clothes which suggested to her peers that she was sexually available. This clothing did not really fit her true personality, which was that of a rather quiet, reserved young woman; rather, it fit an *image* she had of herself as a "with it," fancy-free "swinger." She believed that "a true gentleman" would be able to look beyond her clothing and recognize her true colors. However, few adolescent males could do this, and so she found herself among boys who were attracted to the type of girl she appeared to be.

◆

Younger children can also have significant communication problems associated with their style of dress. Sometimes these problems originate *in* the child—sometimes in the *relationship* between child and parent. The latter is especially the case when style rules reflect and produce a generation gap, as they did with Curt.

It was the first session of family therapy for the Nelsons. They seemed to be a nice family. The Nelsons had two boys—Curt, ten, and Bobby, six. The problems involved Curt. He seemed to have no friends and was not completing his school work. In addition, Curt's mother complained that he would not listen and constantly argued with her at home.

Toward the end of the session, it became apparent that there was a lot of tension between Curt and his mother. To help clarify the source of this tension, the Nelsons were given a task to complete before returning in two days for the next session. Each member of the family was given a stack of ten tokens in one particular color. They were instructed to give a token to another family member whenever that other person did something that was appreciated. As the family left, it was easy to see that the mother thought she would win many more tokens than anyone else.

When the family returned for the next session, it was obvious that, if anything, the tension between Curt and his mother had intensified. When this was noted, the mother began to explain, in an angry tone, what had happened. She said since the last session, she had gotten up early, laid out the clothes for each family member, and cooked a fantastic breakfast. When the father came to breakfast, he gave her a token. When the youngest child came to breakfast, he gave her a token. However, when Curt came to breakfast, he didn't give her a token. As the mother related this incident she became even angrier than she had been before. As she repeated how she had gone to the extra effort of laying out Curt's clothes, she was so angry that she didn't hear Curt say, "That's it!" She went on for a while before finally reacting to her son.

"That's what?!" replied mother indignantly.

"You put out that balloon shirt," Curt said, "and all the kids made fun of me. They always make fun of me because of how I dress."

His mother seemed genuinely surprised by this revelation, and we spent the majority of the session discussing the relationship between Curt and his mother. It seemed that Curt's mother had been brought up with two sisters and really didn't know what little boys wear. Further, she didn't want to admit that Curt's adolescence was just around the corner, and so she dressed him as a little boy. This created significant problems in his relationships with his peers. At the end of the session, both Curt and his mother understood one another better, and Curt and his parents went to buy some age-appropriate clothes for the boys.

◆

Not all problems involving style of dress can be cleared up as easily as Curt's. For example, in some families, younger children must wear "hand-me-downs" or clothing that is ill-fitting or out of style. While most adults empathize with these situations, children are less able and sometimes less willing to do this. Like it or not, the concept of a "nerd," "geek," or "loser" is, all too frequently, intimately tied to clothes and how they are worn. Advising families with limited budgets about adjusting their finances in order to meet their child's social needs must be done sensitively and with tact. It must be made clear that *clothing which is more "in style" need not be more expensive.* Many homemakers' magazines and sewing shops carry relatively easy patterns for stylish clothing. Similarly, there is a wide range of discount stores which offer "designer" clothing at reasonable prices. Creative parents can also be very resourceful; for example, when dancers' warm-ups were popular among adolescent girls, some parents made them by cutting the sleeves off of old sweaters. Other parents have improved their children's wardrobes by taking imaginative looks at the clothing *in their own closets* and adapting some items to the current teen styles. We have even seen teachers set up dressing, hairstyle, and personal hygiene groups in schools where, in a club-like atmosphere, children can learn to maximize their resources.

> *L*ike it or not, the concept of a "nerd," "geek," or "loser" is, all too frequently, intimately tied to clothes and how they are worn.

In addition to those with limited income, there are those children and adults who can afford to dress fashionably, but don't do so because they don't have a clear sense of how their appearance impresses others. They may not be aware of the potential negative connotations of wearing their pants too high or too low or of wearing out-of-style clothes. Such children are typically unaware of how they affect others, and it is difficult to say anything to them for fear of appearing "rude" or hurting their feelings. However, when feedback is given in a sensitive manner by teachers and parents, we have seen that most of these individuals are eager to improve their dressing patterns. Such feedback is most effective when the child is progressing and dressing more appropriately. A simple, "You really look nice today," can go a long way in helping a child to recognize the power of his or her style. Focusing solely on the negative can have markedly destructive effects, especially in young adolescents.

In addition to makeup, hairstyle, and some of the other objectic patterns we have described, the shape and form of one's body has also become an important channel for nonverbal communication. In recent years, great emphasis has been placed on how people maintain themselves physically. A glance at the number of runners, walkers, swimmers, body builders, and other amateur athletes in America should add convincing testimony to the importance of what we tell others about ourselves via weight, muscle development and agility. Further, body development can be used to help dyssemic children. Consider what happened to Jamal, a young child who was school-phobic and had a speech impediment.

Jamal, age 11, was a slightly built child who had a two-year history of school avoidance. Almost every day, he and his parents went through a tearful struggle at the breakfast table when Jamal insisted that he did not feel well enough to go to school. Typically, his parents insisted that he go, and he would, weeping quietly on the school bus. His tears would not stop until 9:00 or 9:30 A.M., after which he seemed to be able to function adequately. Jamal had few friends, and was the butt of many jokes and much ridicule due to his uncontrollable crying. Finding that there were no reasons for his phobia beyond his terrible insecurity at school, we recommended that Jamal begin a personalized weight training program. Weight training and noncompetitive running or swimming are excellent self-esteem builders because if one merely practices, one will get better and better.

With the help of a friendly instructor, Jamal slowly began to build himself up until he was seen in the clinic one year later. At that time, his psychologist was amazed at the difference. Here was a boy wearing a tight T-shirt which showed off a bulging chest and impressive arms. He was smiling and confident. He reported that he was no longer afraid to go to school and that many of the other boys were friendlier to him now. He stated that he knew that he was stronger than almost everyone in his class, but that he would never use his strength for fighting unless he had to. His instructor had instilled that code in him. Jamal's school phobia had disappeared, and he no longer was communicating vulnerability and fear. His expressive objectic communication was much improved, as were his social and academic experiences.

◆

Jamal's problem was solved because caring adults teamed up with him to help Jamal overcome his phobia and improve his self-esteem.

Body Odor: A Difficult Problem in Objectic Communication

While clothing can clearly be a difficult thing to talk about with children, an even knottier issue is body odor. As liberal and accepting as teachers and peers try to be, it is almost impossible to ignore a child whose personal hygiene habits are so poor that he or she smells badly. In our society, we have come to expect others to have sweet breath, clean hair, and fresh-smelling skin. These elements of hygiene are often seen as basic to social interactions, be they at home, work, play, or school. People tend to avoid a child who is remiss in the area of hygiene. Adults are usually polite in such circumstances and will rarely, if ever, mention the problem. As we noted when we talked about clothing, however, children are not always so polite. Often they will call children with unattractive body odors by hurtful names and will mock them. The result is painful to think about and to watch. Consider what happened to Rusty as a result of his objectic dyssemia.

Rusty came from a middle-class family. He had four siblings and lived in what could best be termed as a "chaotic" house. Each morning, Rusty's parents and their five children all had to get ready in about an hour. With only two bathrooms in the house, the situation was one of limited resources. Being the next to youngest, Rusty often wound up not getting to wash well, brush his teeth, or even change his underwear before he was called down to breakfast. On Mondays, he was typically well dressed and groomed, but by midweek he began to smell badly (from lack of showering and three-day-old underthings).

The school children would play games around him, trying to give him hints about his body odor. One child would ask, "What stinks around here?" Others would ask, "What happens to metal when it gets wet? It gets rusty!" They would also avoid Rusty and would never pick him as a partner or team member. Rusty's teacher knew what the problem was and tried to help him. She asked the gym teacher to teach all of the boys about personal hygiene, hoping that, before he was singled out, Rusty would get the message. However, teaching Rusty to take care of himself was not enough, since he simply did not have enough time in the mornings to do so. A visit from his teacher for a caring conversation with Rusty's parents (who were more than willing to help once they were made aware of the situation) resulted in some simple scheduling changes at their house which led to a cleaner, happier, and more widely accepted young man.

◆

Although rather easily solved, Rusty's dyssemia was due to more than his body odor and unclean clothing. It was also due to his **expressive dyssemia** in this area—the fact that *he was not aware* of the expressive power of his poor personal hygiene. Had he known the teasing was caused by his own body odor, he surely would have corrected it sooner.

As we consider communication through objectics, we need to focus on its use as a receptive language as well as an expressive one. For example, **receptive accuracy** in "reading" style of dress can be an extremely important tool for maintaining a child's safety. We spend a great deal of our time as parents teaching our children about whom to approach and whom to avoid. One of the first things we teach them is that when they are in trouble, they should find a police officer. How are they supposed to identify a police officer? By being able to read the "meaning" expressed through a police uniform.

> E lements of hygiene are often seen as basic to social interactions, be they at home, work, play, or school. People tend to avoid a child who is remiss in the area of personal hygiene.

There are other situations in which understanding style of dress in others is important. If a child is lost and a police officer is unavailable, what sorts of people should the child seek out? Strangers with satanic tattoos on their arms and safety pins through their noses? A man dressed in a business suit? If a child is looking for someone to play baseball with, should he ask a child dressed in a football uniform?

■ **TIPS FOR PARENTS AND TEACHERS** ■
Helping Your Child Develop a Better Sense of Style

1. Because fashion changes so rapidly, parents and teachers should not trust their own instincts or memories regarding what is acceptable, but should observe other children in school, at the shopping malls, on TV shows, in magazines, etc. In this way, adults can establish a child's-eye view of the currently acceptable trends. Do not believe the old adage, "If it was good enough for me, it will be good enough for them." It won't be.

☐

2. Establish a dictionary of "in" styles of dress, hair, jewelry, etc. Have your child create imaginary outfits based upon the dictionary and discuss the "meanings" of these outfits.   In conjunction with this exercise, go through your child's clothing and talk about what each piece "says" and why.

☐

3. Discuss generally, as well as specifically, the importance of personal hygiene as a mode of communication. Go into detail regarding the basic requirements.

☐

4. Watch soap operas or examine magazines. Discuss how styles of dress reveal personalities or feelings.

☐

5. Create age-appropriate situations that would require the child to seek out others for help. Provide pictures of people dressed in different styles and discuss who/which would be appropriate and why.

☐

6. Provide a variety of different types of clothes and "assign" your child a personality or attitude to portray by selecting an outfit. Also use makeup, jewelry, perfumes, deodorants, colognes, etc.

☐

7. Go to a mall and visit various shops. Watch people dressed in various ways and try to guess which stores they might go into or would not go into. Develop this into a game with points and other rewards for accurate "reading" of style-of-dress cues. Discuss the ways in which clothing can help us to know personalities, interests, attitudes, and values.

☐

In combining objectics with all of the other channels of nonverbal language that we have described, it is easy to see that social success is akin to paddling down a rapid river in which rocks or trees may crop up in the water at any moment. If we "read" these obstacles correctly and have the wherewithal to respond to them appropriately, we will continue our journey unscathed; but if we don't see them or we don't know what to do, the danger of tipping over increases. Each of us must be able to "read" nonverbal language correctly and to respond to it appropriately. Further, the signs and cues that we produce for others must be clear and readable and must accurately reflect what we are trying to say. If a child cannot do these things and, from informal observation, appears to suffer from a severe expressive or receptive dyssemia, formal assessment may be necessary to isolate, understand, and remediate the problem. It is to these matters that we now turn.

PART TWO:

PUTTING IT ALL TOGETHER

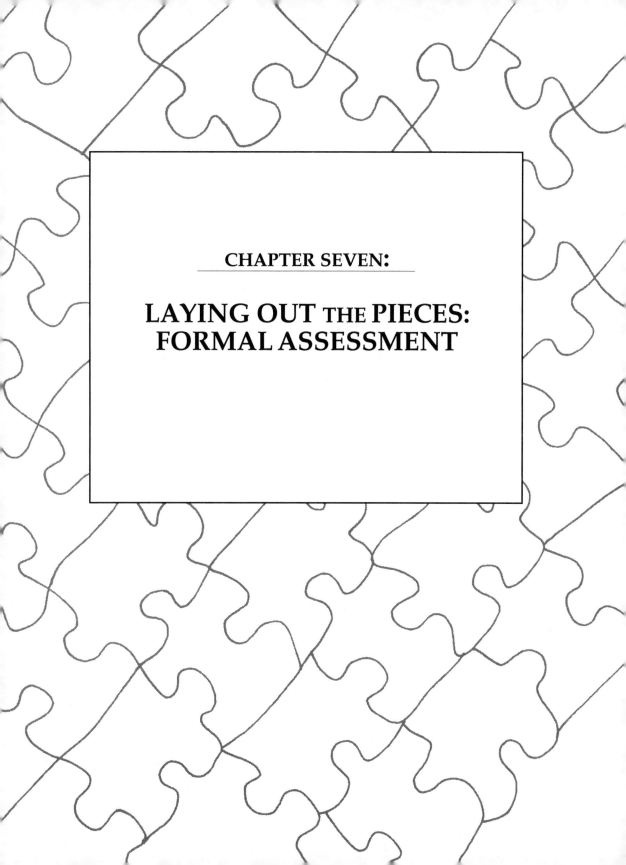

CHAPTER SEVEN:

LAYING OUT THE PIECES: FORMAL ASSESSMENT

LAYING OUT the PIECES: FORMAL ASSESSMENT

We know that there are many socially rejected children and adults who suffer from specific dyssemic problems. Most of the time, the *informal assessment* described in chapters 1 through 6 will yield enough information for you to judge whether your child has dyssemia—a nonverbal communication deficit—and it will give you some idea of how extensive the problem is. However, there are instances in which the informal methods are unsatisfactory, either because the information is inconclusive or because the dyssemia appears so severe or complex that it may require professional attention. In such cases, more *formal assessment* methods may be required to evaluate the form and extent of a dyssemic deficit. Formal assessment allows us to be more certain about the actual presence of dyssemia and more efficient in prescribing remediational—corrective—procedures.

Formal assessment should include general tests which focus on the child's abilities to receive and express nonverbal social information. However, few such tests are available yet. Tests of auditory and visual perception are useful, but they may not sample the various channels—forms—of nonverbal communication closely enough, especially in regard to social interaction. We suggest you work with your professional to explain your child's problem areas so that individualized tests can be developed. To aid you in the search for formal assessors, we have provided an appendix naming organizations that you can contact for help. Keep in mind that any battery—series—of tests to assess nonverbal communication should include tests to evaluate your child's ability to:

1. **discriminate** among nonverbal cues,
2. **identify** the emotions presented in nonverbal communication,
3. **express** the emotions through various nonverbal channels,
4. **apply** nonverbal information to interpret what is happening in diverse conversations.

We will come back to these four abilities, which were originally outlined by Esther Minskoff, when we discuss remediation because they constitute the backbone of our suggested corrective procedures.

We have constructed our own formal assessment instrument (test), the *Diagnostic Analysis of Nonverbal Accuracy* (**DANVA**), which focuses on the major nonverbal communication channels.

> You may find it helpful to modify some of the DANVA procedures for use in your own informal assessment of your child.

We hope it will become one of many such tests concerned with nonverbal communication. While the DANVA is designed as a *formal* assessment instrument for use by professionals, you may find it helpful to modify some of the procedures for use in your own *informal* assessment of your child.

The DANVA is composed of eight subtests: four to measure the ability to *understand*, and four to measure the ability to *send* nonverbal information. These tests cover the most frequently used channels of nonverbal communication: facial expressions, postures, gestures, personal space, and tone of voice. Further, the subtests use the four most commonly encountered emotions—anger, fear, happiness, and sadness—to measure the abilities to receive and send nonverbal information.

1. Understanding Facial Expressions. In this test, a slide projector and forty slides are used. Twenty slides show adult facial expressions, and the other twenty show children's expressions. For both the adult and child expressions, there are four slides—two males and two females—for each of the four emotions (anger, fear, happiness, and sadness). There are an additional four slides that show no particular emotion. The slides are shown for one second, and the child taking the test states which emotion is being expressed.

2. Sending Facial Expressions. This test consists of eight trials. The child should be sitting in a comfortable chair, ten feet away from a videocamera. He or she is then read one of eight descriptive situations by the examiner and asked to express the proper emotion. For example, the examiner would say, "You have received a birthday present that you have always wanted. You feel happy. Show me a happy face." The child's expression is then videotaped. There are two descriptive examples for each of the four basic emotional states (anger, fear, happiness, and sadness). Rating scales that range from 1 (not accurate) to 3 (very accurate) are used to judge the child's abilities to convey the appropriate emotions. Important here is the accuracy of emotion as well as the accuracy of intensity of emotion; it is possible for a child to correctly communicate a particular emotion while overstating or understating that emotion with the improper intensity.

3. Understanding Gestures. There are twelve slides of a model using gestures that reflect the four basic emotions (anger, fear, happiness and sadness). Each of the four emotions is represented by three slides. The slides are shown for one second, and the child must indicate which emotion is being expressed through the particular gesture.

4. Sending Gestures. In this test, there are twelve trials—three for each of the four basic emotions. The child is seated in a comfortable chair ten feet from a video camera, and is instructed to use only his or her hands and arms to send a particular emotion (anger, for example). The child's gestures are videotaped and rated for accuracy.

5. Understanding Tone of Voice. There are sixteen trials in which a model says the following sentence, "I am going out of the room now, and I will be back later." Each time, the model varies the voice tone to reflect one of the four basic emotions (anger, fear, happiness, and sadness).

6. Sending Tone of Voice. There are eight trials in this test. The child is seated in a comfortable chair next to a tape recorder's microphone (or a videocamera with a microphone). The child is then handed a sheet of paper upon which is printed, in block letters, the following sentence, "I am going to get my bike now and go for a ride." The child is given time to practice reading the sentence. The examiner then describes one of eight situations. The child responds by reading the sentence and inflecting the appropriate emotion for the described situation. For example, the cue could be, "You have have found out that you have won a nice prize in a contest. You feel happy. Say the sentence in such a way that you sound happy." There are two trials for each of the four emotions. The recordings are subjected to similar ratings as those used to rate facial expressions and gestures.

7. Understanding Postures. In this test, there are twelve slides of a person showing various postures. The postures reflect the four basic emotions (anger, fear, happiness and sadness). Each emotion is represented by three slides. Care was taken to hide the face of the person portraying the posture. The slides are shown for one second, and the child must state which emotion is being expressed through posture. Note: *the test for sending postures is still undergoing field evaluation, and therefore cannot yet be described.*

8. Sending Personal Space. To measure personal space, the Comfortable Interpersonal Distance Scale is used. People taking the test are given a piece of paper with a representation of a room on it similar to that shown in figure 7.1. From the center of the room, eight lines of equal distance (eighty millimeters) radiate out in a circle.

Fig. 7.1. COMFORTABLE INTERPERSONAL DISTANCE SCALE

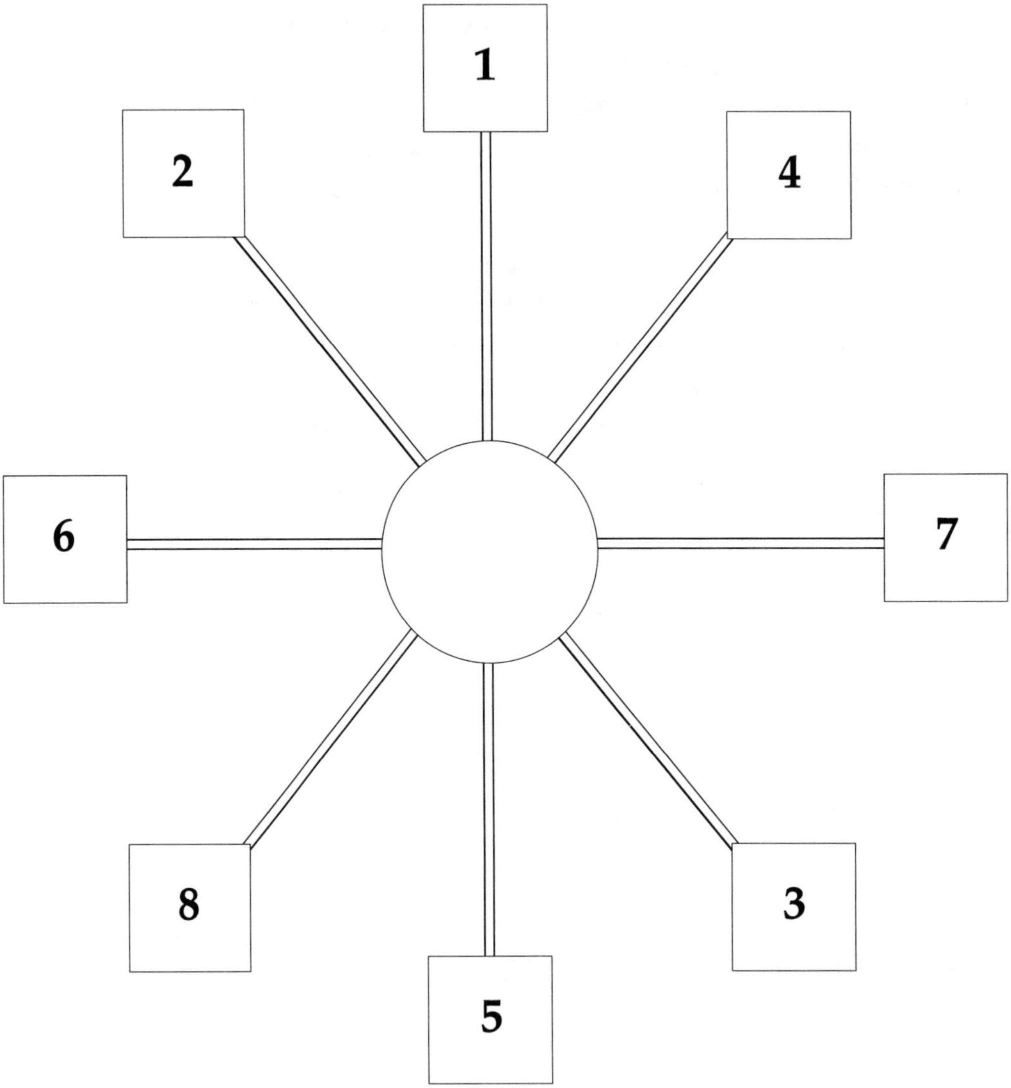

Children taking the test are asked to imagine that they are standing in the center of the room and that each line leads to a different door. Further, they are asked to imagine that they are facing door 1 (the number at the top of the page). The examiner then describes an imaginary person at door 1, and says that the described person is going to walk toward the center of the room (where the child is "standing"). The child is to make a mark on the line where he or she would like the imaginary person to stop. After making the mark, the child is asked to imagine turning to the right and facing door 2. The tester then describes a different imaginary person at that door.

The examiner can use all eight doors and describe any sort of individual desired. For example, the person could be a stranger who is the same age and same gender as the child taking the test, or the described individual could be the president of the United States. For the DANVA the following individuals were described:

◆ a stranger who is the same age and sex as you

■ a stranger who is the same age and opposite sex as you

◆ a stranger who is five years younger than you and the same sex

■ a stranger who is five years older than you and the same sex

◆ your best friend

■ your mother

◆ a school teacher who is a stranger to you

■ the president of the United States.

The interpersonal distance between the center point and the marks made for each described individual is measured. The distances chosen for the imaginary people are then compared to the distances chosen by the child's peers. This gives information as to whether the child's distances are greater or less than those chosen by most others. Note: *the subtest for understanding interpersonal space is still undergoing field evaluation, and therefore cannot yet be described.*

◇

When used by professionals who have access to the DANVA norms, scores from the eight subtests can produce a profile of a child's nonverbal processing abilities. DANVA norms are based upon the testing of several thousand children and allow for the evaluation of a child's performance as compared to that of his or her peers. For example, the average fifth-grader can recognize twenty-nine out of a possible thirty-two facial expressions correctly. If the child we test is a fifth grader, and he or she correctly identifies nineteen faces, we know the child's performance is much below that of other fifth graders. Further, if the person we test is twenty-one years old and he or she only identifies nineteen faces correctly, we know that this person is performing at a level much below that of fifth graders, let alone his or her adult peers.

For some children, formal or informal assessment may show that their dyssemia is very specific and encapsulated. Consider Gary's problem:

Gary was a compactly built twelve-year-old. He was being evaluated because he was performing below expectations in school. Among other tests, he was given the DANVA. He performed at or above the level of his peers on seven of the eight subtests. However, on the facial expressions subtest, he scored substantially lower than his peers. Gary demonstrated a *specific* nonverbal processing deficit. Although his records suggested that he was not experiencing many relationship problems, the low score in understanding facial expressions indicated that he may be at risk in the future. Since Gary stands on the brink of adolescence, when mistakes in reading the facial expressions of others can have serious, negative consequences, it would certainly be prudent to remediate this specific difficulty before any significant problems begin.

◆

In contrast to *specific* dyssemias are combined deficiencies, *complex* dyssemias, whose impacts are more diverse and potentially more serious. Consider what Meg may be up against.

Meg is a very quiet child of nine. She was being tested because her school work was suffering and she didn't seem to have any friends. Meg scored substantially lower than her peers on six of the eight DANVA subtests. In fact, on facial expressions and tone of voice, she scored much lower than her peers on both understanding and sending emotions. This set of scores suggests that Meg was suffering from generalized dyssemia. Beyond the problems she was already experiencing, these scores suggested that she was at high risk for developing more extensive problems in the future. Also, just because Meg is a quiet person doesn't mean she was happy and satisfied with the way things were going.

◆

Causes of Dyssemia

Although the DANVA can indicate strengths and weaknesses in nonverbal communication, it does not identify the source or sources of dyssemia. With Meg, the subtests found her dyssemia, but they did not cite the root of her problems. We believe there are three major ways in which a child can develop dyssemia: 1. a **lack of the appropriate situations and experiences** which allow for proper learning of nonverbal language; 2. a **brain dysfunction** which results in a social perception learning disability; 3. **emotional difficulties** producing anxiety or depression which prevent the proper learning of nonverbal language.

The lack of opportunity to learn the nonverbal language, we suspect, plays a part in the great majority of dyssemia cases. In such cases, children have the neurological ability to learn nonverbal skills and aren't encumbered by any acute or chronic emotional problems, but they simply didn't have the opportunity to experience the kinds of situations necessary for appropriate learning of nonverbal communication.

For instance, a child may be raised in a family where certain negative emotions, such as anger, are simply not communicated or, if communicated, are not identified. While a child in this situation may have the emotional and cognitive ability to recognize and send anger through nonverbal channels, his or her family does not offer enough opportunity for the appropriate learning to take place. If such a child spends most of the time at home, chances are that he or she probably will experience relatively few problems. However, if such a child must interact with others outside the house in situations where it's important to properly respond to signals indicating anger, there's a good chance of interpersonal confusion. Further, the child's family may not even be aware of their own nonverbal deficiencies.

> There are three major ways in which a child can develop dyssemia:
> 1. a lack of the appropriate situations and experiences;
> 2. a brain dysfunction;
> 3. emotional difficulties.

Lack of appropriate learning experiences probably plays a significant part in the adjustment difficulties that may be experienced by immigrants to the United States. These immigrant children are at risk for developing nonverbal communication problems. Consider what happened to Da Song:

He was just about as cute as a seven-year-old boy could be— dark features, with big, beautiful eyes and black, shiny hair. Da was Vietnamese, and he was being evaluated at the request of the school he was attending. There was concern on the school's part that he was not fitting in even though he was doing well academically. Da seemed to be very different from the other children; it was not his appearance, but it was the way he handled himself nonverbally. When others talked to him, he held his head down, and when he spoke to others, he looked somewhere around their shoe tops. When the other children approached him with big smiles, Da would immediately bow his head down, and, because of that response, he was unable to take notice of the friendship being offered to him. Further, the other children only saw what appeared to be very serious expressions on Da's face. Thus, he was alienating himself from others, and he didn't realize it.

After talking with Da's teachers and his family, as well as with a Vietnamese psychologist, we realized that Da's nonverbal language *was* appropriate behavior in his homeland. In Vietnam, there is little emphasis on reading facial expressions. In fact, it is considered to be rude. We worked out a program for helping Da and his parents become familiar with American nonverbal culture. Because he always had the ability to process nonverbal information, it didn't take long for Da to successfully complete a remediation program focused on reading and sending facial expressions.

◆

Da provided us with a good illustration of how important family and the related subculture are in the learning of nonverbal language. Since parents are the primary teachers of nonverbal language, it follows that overuse or underuse of a particular nonverbal behavior by them leaves a child inadequately prepared for the use of nonverbal language outside of the home. This reminds us of Bill.

Bill is a child who rarely communicated any sort of emotion in his facial expression, except when he was angry. Then we met Bill's parents. As they sat down to discuss Bill, we noticed that they also expressed little emotion in their facial expressions, except when they were angry with us. When we pointed out Bill's limited facial expressions, they agreed that Bill needed to be more expressive! Again—consistent with the attributes of nonverbal language—the parents were unaware that they possessed a nonverbal communication deficit—dyssemia—similar to their son's.

◆

Our own clinical experiences suggest that the foundation for learning nonverbal social communication is developed within families. Further, as Johnson and Myklebust have pointed out, since nonverbal language is learned indirectly, an incomplete foundation may allow certain types and processes of nonverbal language to be "skipped" in the child's nonverbal education; such children are therefore at a higher risk for developing problems which may well lead to social rejection.

In addition to those dyssemic children whose problems stem from lack of learning, there are also a number whose troubles originate in some inherent or acquired brain dysfunction. According to Johnson and Myklebust, depending upon which area of the brain is affected, various types of learning disabilities (such as in reading or math) may develop. Johnson and Myklebust termed one of these learning disabilities "social perception disability," a pattern characterized by difficulties in responding appropriately to social/emotional cues. According to them, due to a subtle disruption of brain functioning, individuals with this kind of learning disability cannot learn or use the information necessary to perceive themselves in relation to their environment and the behavior of others.

Children who have such a brain dysfunction fail to learn the association between nonverbal cues such as facial expressions and *feeling states* such as anger. To Johnson and Myklebust, the failure to learn this association makes social perception learning disabilities one of the most debilitating of all the learning disabilities because they prevent one from learning the basics of adaptive behavior. In other words, a child is unable to carry what he or she has learned from one situation into another. Further, Byron Rourke suggested that a certain subtype of biologically based nonverbal learning disability predisposes children to the development of depression. Consider Jimmy's troubles on the school playground.

Watching Jimmy on the playground was painful. One of us had been asked to clinically evaluate this ten-year-old who seemed to have no friends and, although he had an above-average IQ, was not achieving up to grade level.

Jimmy was in line awaiting his turn to participate in the playground game under way. As the line moved forward, one could see small equal places between the children in line except for the place between Jimmy and the child in front of him. As the line continued to move, Jimmy was either too close to the child ahead of him, or he stood so far off it was hard to tell if he was in line or not. Even after the child ahead continually pushed Jimmy away, Jimmy could not seem to remember, and within a moment or two, he was back nudging the child again. It was easy to see why Jimmy had trouble fitting in.

◆

Jimmy was clearly shown that he was standing too close to the other child, but only a few minutes later, he seemed unable to apply the knowledge. It almost seemed as though Jimmy believed the rule about standing too close was only for that instant, but not the next.

It has been our experience that there are certainly some children and adults whose social rejection problems stem from neurological sources. However, we have come to believe that, to a much greater degree, the *dyssemia we have linked to social rejection is more likely to emerge as a result of non-biologically based causes* such as the previously described lack of learning opportunities as well as emotional factors.

> The dyssemia we have linked to social rejection is more likely to emerge as a result of non-biologically based causes.

Emotional difficulties such as being overly anxious may short-circuit the learning of nonverbal information. It has long been known that emotional traumas, if they are intense enough, as in the death or illness of a parent, can shut down many learning mechanisms in children, including those necessary for learning nonverbal social information. It is also important to realize that people define for themselves what is traumatic; what may not seem very stressful to one child may be an emotional trauma to another. We all have our own unique personal vulnerabilities and even single incidents have the capacity to seriously disrupt the processing of basic nonverbal information.

Besides the impact of a single intense emotional event, prolonged stress is also known to disrupt the learning and processing of nonverbal communication. When under stress, children and adults attempt to mobilize their psychological and physiological resources to deal with the source of the stress. One way individuals try to deal with stress is to *select* what they pay attention to in order to take in only the kinds of information that will reduce anxiety. For example, if a child has a sick parent, he or she may not listen to stories in school about Dick and Jane going to the hospital. Similarly, children may miss or distort other kinds of information in an attempt to reduce stress or anxiety. High levels of stress can cause a child's behavior to become more disorganized and can hamper nonverbal communication skills. Thus, children reared in highly stressful environments may well be candidates for social rejection as a result of being dyssemic. It is also possible that children who are failing in school, either because of a "traditional" learning disability in reading or math or because they do not have the intellectual ability to keep up with their peers, may experience the kinds of anxiety and stress that could also then produce dyssemia.

Fig. 7.2
A "traditional" learning disability may also cause sufficient stress and anxiety to produce dyssemia.

Further, children who are depressed or inordinately anxious cannot fully attend to the nonverbal signals in their environment. Due to their psychological difficulties, they may unknowingly produce nonverbal signs that do not accurately reflect their feeling states or needs. The result, in either case, can be interpersonal difficulties that only serve to make their emotional problems worse.

◇

Once you've completed the informal or formal assessment process and identified a dyssemic pattern, formal or informal remediation (corrective treatments) should be addressed. Informal remediation not only can but should be done by parents and teachers; they are the agents of choice for this kind of learning. We will now move on to remediation.

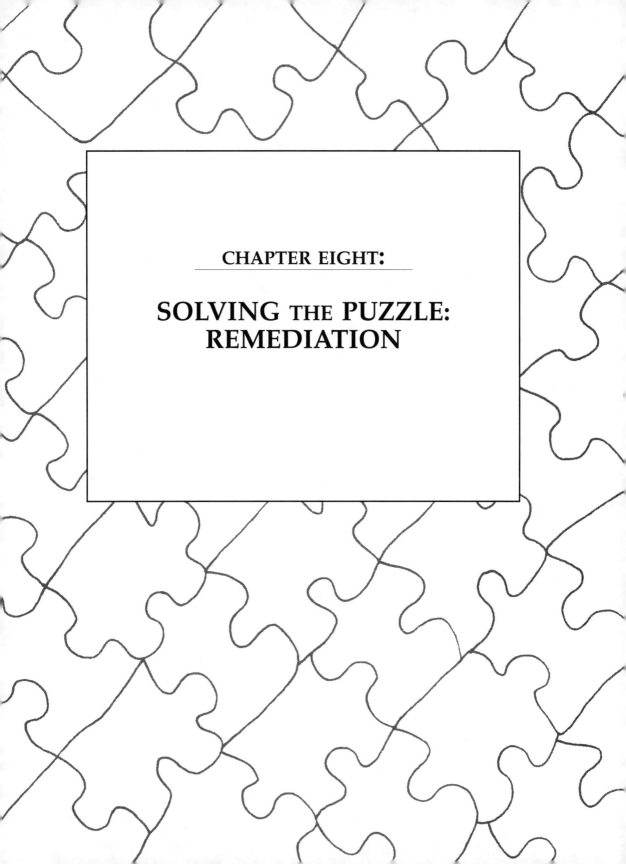

CHAPTER EIGHT:

SOLVING THE PUZZLE: REMEDIATION

SOLVING THE PUZZLE: REMEDIATION

◇

Whether you use informal or formal remediation, remember that you are trying to help a child who is suffering from a deficit that has probably lowered his or her self-esteem and made the child feel as though there is little or no connection between behavior and its impact. We want to make the child aware of dyssemia, improve nonverbal skills, and thereby improve the child's self-worth by allowing him or her to see the connection between behavior and its consequences. Because a dyssemic child has experienced failure, you should be supportive of the child's efforts toward self-improvement. Be your child's tutor. Engage the child in the remediation process; make it a cooperative venture with a positive outcome. Clearly explain what you are trying to do, and encourage your child to ask as many questions as necessary. We want the child to be comfortable with what we are asking him or her to do. At the end of the remediation process, we hope your child will be a more confident individual.

Informal Remediation: Tutoring

As with informal assessment, tips for informal remediation—tutoring—have been placed throughout the book. Some tips, like charades, can be used to help children with expressive deficits (by having them perform the charades) and children with receptive deficits (by having them guess the charades). Other tips, like placing tape around the desk of a "space invader" to help the child be aware of where his or her personal space ends and another's begins, are more specific to a particular nonverbal behavior. In either case, parents and teachers try to help a child learn to associate particular feelings with particular nonverbal behaviors by explaining the connection between them. This goal is consistent with the remediation recommendations made by Johnson and Myklebust, who believe that a child needs to establish these associations by direct learning. A child with nonverbal communication problems who has failed to learn the accurate use of nonverbal language indirectly now needs to be directly taught what he or she has missed.

Help a child learn to associate particular feelings with particular nonverbal behaviors by explaining the connection between them.

Formal Remediation

While our formal remediation method was developed for use by mental health professionals, you may wish to adapt for your own informal use some of the remediation procedures presented in this section. We will give you some tips on how to make modifications along the way.

Our remediation procedures are based on the work of Minskoff and Johnson and Myklebust, and on our own clinical work with teachers, parents, and children. These procedures can and should be modified to fit the needs of a particular child. The procedures are based on theory, research, and experience suggesting that:

1. people who have trouble processing nonverbal information tend to have problems in relating to others;

2. nonverbal social processing skills can be taught with appropriate instructions;

3. improved nonverbal processing skills translate into better interpersonal relationships.

As we mentioned earlier, remediation should be administered within a helpful and supportive environment. Since dyssemic children are attempting to learn associations that are difficult for them, it is important for the *remediator— tutor*—to create an atmosphere in which failures are accepted and successes are reinforced; *the process of learning should be fun.*

The time taken to complete remediation varies widely. Depending on their age and the extensiveness of the dyssemia, children will differ in the speed at which they learn nonverbal social processing skills. Do not rush the learning process; make sure your child is enjoying what is going on. Starting small and making sure that the child feels good is more important than the pace. After each stage of the remediation process, make sure that the child has taken hold of the new information and made it a part of his or her daily processing before moving on.

> The time taken to complete remediation varies widely. Do not rush the learning process. Make sure that the child has taken hold of the new information and made it a part of his or her daily processing before moving on.

The Four Stages of Remediation

Before we give you an extensive example of the remediation process, which you can adapt to suit your child's needs, we want to make you aware that *a successful remediation program must take place in four stages, with each stage including three crucial subprocesses.*

The remediation stages should take place in order of difficulty. Remediation begins with the simplest stage—*discrimination* among nonverbal language cues—and it ends with the most complex—*application* of nonverbal language to social situations. The four ascending levels of nonverbal processing ability taught in this program are as follows:

LEVEL 1: **DISCRIMINATION** OF NONVERBAL CUES. At this level, a child is taught to discriminate (discern) whether nonverbal cues are *similar to* or *different from* one another. To accomplish this goal, children are taught to pay attention to the critical elements of nonverbal cues so that differences become easier to see. For example, a child may be presented with two facial expressions which communicate the same emotion—happiness— or two different emotions—happiness and sadness. In each instance, the child is asked, "Are these expressions the same or are they different?"

LEVEL 2: UNDERSTANDING THE **MEANING** OF NONVERBAL CUES. At this level, the learning becomes more complex, and children are taught to interpret nonverbal cues. They must respond to descriptions of the feelings associated with nonverbal cues. For example, the remediator will ask, "Is this a happy face?" and the child must answer accurately. Because it asks individuals to *identify* emotions, Level 2 tasks are more demanding than those at Level 1, which only require the child to indicate whether two or more cues are alike or different.

LEVEL 3: MEANINGFUL **EXPRESSION** OF SPECIFIC NON-VERBAL CUES. At this level of furthered complexity, a child is required to name or describe a nonverbal cue or feeling. Unlike Level 2, in which the child is only asked to agree or disagree with the named emotion (Is this a happy face?), a child at Level 3 must name the feeling reflected in the nonverbal cue. Thus the tutor will ask, "What feeling does this facial expression show?" To answer, the child must have acquired the skills of Levels 1 and 2—he or she must be able to discriminate and understand nonverbal cues.

LEVEL 4: **APPLICATION** OF NONVERBAL CUES TO SOCIAL SITUATIONS: At this final and most complex level of nonverbal communication, children learn through such activities as role playing and verbal problem solving (describing how they must deal with various situations). They learn to discriminate the nonverbal cues at work in a particular situation, relate them to the *verbal* responses, and apply what is learned to future interactions. We will give a practical example of this a little later on. At Level 4, there is a special emphasis on learning to recognize and express *negative* nonverbal cues because they are the ones most detrimental to effective interactions.

Above we have described the four main levels of remediation. Tutors should take children through these four stages in a careful and thorough manner and at each child's own pace. In the process of so doing, the tutor should ensure that the following three subprocesses occur in each stage.

SUBPROCESS 1: As we have suggested elsewhere, the first subprocess requires that children become **aware** of their deficits as well as what it will take to remediate them.

Subprocess 2: Once a child becomes aware of the necessary components for remediation, it is crucial that he or she **practice** these components. Further, the child should **verbalize** this nonverbal process. By stating the connections between nonverbal cues and emotions, the child becomes aware of the link between communication channels and social situations. Appropriate reactions will then become natural responses of the child.

Subprocess 3: After practicing and learning the less complex components of nonverbal communication in simple situations, a child must then **apply** his or her learning to other and more complex circumstances in order to generalize what has been learned.

As children repeat the process of *awareness*, *practice*, and *application*, the accurate use of nonverbal information should become more natural and automatic.

Example: *Remediation for Facial Expression Dyssemia*

What follows is an example of how we would apply the four stages of remediation to *one type* of dyssemia (we'll use facial expressions). These procedures can be easily applied to any of the other nonverbal areas and can be modified or added to by parents and teachers. In fact, many of the activities included in the facial expressions example were contributed by parents and teachers. We thank them for their contributions and urge you, as well, to develop procedures that may be helpful in reaching your child's goals.

LEVEL 1: DISCRIMINATION OF FACIAL EXPRESSIONS

The goal at this level is to teach whether the faces that a child looks at are similar to or different from one another. At this level, we don't care whether a child can tell **what** is being communicated by facial expressions; our only concern is that the child can tell whether facial expressions are similar to or different from one another. If a child cannot discriminate facial expressions from one another, he or she cannot learn any of the other more complex nonverbal language tasks.

Most of the procedures at this level will ask the child to verbalize whether the faces are similar or different. When your child makes a mistake, explain the error, and urge him or her to verbally repeat your explanation. Here are a number of ways to improve a child's ability to discriminate among facial expressions. Different exercises will be useful with different children, and they need not be used in any particular order. Much will depend on the child, the tutor, and the relationship between them.

A. The materials used are pictures taken from magazines and newspapers. Try to include facial expressions depicting anger, fear, happiness, and sadness (of males and females as well as of adults and children). Anger, fear, happiness, and sadness are believed by many to be core or basic emotions, but other emotions may also be addressed.

Show two or more of the pictures and ask, "Are they similar or are they different?" Include a variety of people and the four major feelings (anger, fear, happiness and sadness). Here are some comparisons:

- ◆ Use two adults. First use two males, then two females, then use a male and a female (to be sure the child can make accurate judgments across the genders)

- ◆ Use two children (two males, then two females, and then mixed genders again)

◆ Use an adult and a child—two males, two females, male adult and female child, female
adult and male child (to be sure children can
make accurate judgments across age and
gender).

Another way to use these pictures is to put them face down
on a table and play a game of concentration with your child. Many
children are already familiar with the game and will have some
idea of the rules. If not, tell the child to match the faces on the basis
of their similar expressions. Turn over two cards at a time and see
whether the cards have like expressions. If not, turn the faces over
again. When the child finds facial expressions that match, he or
she gets to remove the cards from the board and keep them. The
game continues until all of the expressions are accurately matched.
When a child makes a mistake, the remediator/tutor points out
how the faces are different and has the child verbally repeat the
reasons why the facial expressions don't match.

B. Using the same materials as in A, show the child a picture
of a facial expression and have him or her attempt to make a facial
expression that is (1) similar to, or (2) different from the one in the
picture. Present photographs of males and females and of adults
and children for each of the four emotions (anger, fear, happiness
and sadness). Vary this exercise in the following ways:

■ Have the child look in a mirror to see whether his
or her facial expression is (1) the same or (2)
different from the one in the picture. When the
child makes mistakes, point out the reasons for
the errors and have the child verbalize these
reasons so that he or she can become aware of

what makes facial expressions similar to or different from one another.

■ Using a Polaroid camera, take a photograph of the child as he or she attempts to show each of the four emotions. These photographs can then be compared to the newspaper or magazine pictures which were originally used to represent those emotions. Again, the question should be asked, "Is your photograph similar to or different from the original photograph?" (TIP: The photographs can be kept and used in other phases of the remediation. Another tip: Let the child pick out one of the photographs to keep as a memento.)

■ Using a videocamera, photograph the child as he or she gives the designated facial expression for each of the four emotions. Use the video of the child's facial expressions and compare it to the original photograph and ask the child, again, if it is similar to or different from the original photograph. (TIP: The videos can be kept and used in other phases of the remediation.)

C. The tutor makes a facial expression for each of the four emotions. After each facial expression, the child is asked to make a facial expression that is either (1) similar to or (2) different from that shown by the tutor. There are any number of ways to make this comparison. The easiest is to use mirrors. Videotaping also is effective.

D. The tutor places four pictures of facial expressions, each representing one of the four emotions, on a table. Then the tutor makes a facial expression that is similar to or different from each picture. The child is asked to look at the photograph and then at the tutor's facial expression to conclude whether they are similar to or different from one another.

LEVEL 2: UNDERSTANDING THE SOCIAL MEANINGS OF FACIAL EXPRESSIONS

Once a child has learned to discriminate facial expressions, he or she can move up to *Level 2, where the child will learn to associate a particular feeling with its appropriate facial expression.* At Level 2, a child is provided with the *names* of feelings, and then is shown different facial expressions. The child is then asked whether the named feelings match the shown expressions.

Children are encouraged to verbalize the judgment process—explain what information they used to arrive at the decision that an emotion was or was not associated with a particular facial expression.

Throughout the training at this level, children are encouraged to *verbalize the judgment process,* (explain what information they used to arrive at the decision that an emotion was or was not associated with a particular facial expression). When a child makes an error, the tutor verbally describes the basis for the error (such as pointing out that the mouth is down-turned, indicating sadness rather than happiness). In this way, the child understands why he or she may have made the mistake. The child is asked to verbally repeat the explanation.

The following is a selection of exercises designed to develop the ability to understand the meanings of facial expressions. As with Level 1 exercises, these may be used in any order and should be adapted to the special needs of the child or tutor.

A. The tutor places a picture of a particular facial expression (these can be the same pictures used for Level 1) on a table and asks, "Is this facial expression a happy one?" The child then responds by agreeing or disagreeing with the statement. If possible, have the child respond both verbally and nonverbally— that is, nod his or her head appropriately to go along with the yes or no verbal response. If the child is correct, the next picture is placed on the table. However, if the child is incorrect, the tutor helps the child to identify where he or she may have been in error and to verbalize the basis for the error. The tutor goes through pictures of males and females, adults and children, for the emotions of anger, fear, happiness and sadness.

B. The tutor makes facial expressions to reflect each of the four emotions and asks the child to identify the emotion being expressed. (For example, "Is this a happy facial expression?")

C. The tutor asks the child to make particular facial expressions in front of a mirror to reflect each of the four emotions (for example, "Show/give me a happy expression"). One modification of this approach is to photograph the child as he or she produces each of the four facial expressions reflecting the basic emotions. Then, place each photograph on the table and ask your child, "Which is the sad person?"

D. Use video replays of television programs. Stop the action and focus the child's attention on a particular character's face. Then ask, "Is this person's facial expression _____ ?" Work with each of the four emotions at least once.

E. The tutor places four or more pictures of facial expressions on a table and asks the child to pick out the one that is _____ (angry, afraid, happy or sad).

F. The tutor chooses a magazine that contains several facial expressions of adults and children. The tutor and the child page through the magazine. The tutor asks the child to "find a _____ face," naming each of the four emotions in turn. One modification of this approach is to have the tutor point out a particular face and ask, "Is this a _____ face?"—again naming each emotion in turn.

LEVEL 3: MEANINGFUL USAGE OF FACIAL EXPRESSIONS

When a child has mastered Levels 1 and 2, it is time to move to the more difficult task of mastering Level 3. At this level, a child is required to produce the name of the emotion associated with a facial expression. In Level 2, the tutor named the emotion and child was required to answer. However, at Level 3, a child must *produce* the name or give a verbal description of a particular facial expression, rather than have the tutor give the name. Here are a number of exercises designed to improve a child's ability to interpret facial information meaningfully. You may find that Exercises A, B, and C are somewhat easier and more basic than D and E, but as usual the order and selection of the exercises needs to be "tailored" to fit each child.

A. The tutor places pictures of facial expressions on a table and asks the child to tell which emotion is being shown by each face. The child must respond to each of the four emotions as shown by males and females, adults and children. Again, as is the case with all levels of remediation, when an error is made the tutor points out and explains the mistake. Then, the child is encouraged to repeat the explanation. (For example, "It's an angry face because the lips are tight and the eyes are squinty.")

B. The tutor selects a magazine with pictures of people's faces. While paging through it, point to various faces and ask the child to state which emotion is being expressed. Make sure that the facial expressions are chosen to reflect each of the four emotions for males and females, adults and children.

C. The tutor makes facial expressions reflecting each of the four emotions and asks the child to say what emotion is being expressed. (TIP: Be sure to vary the intensity of your facial expressions from slight to great. You may want to practice in front of a mirror so that you're sure of the type and intensity of facial expression you're sending. Further, you may want to do this exercise in front of a mirror with the child for comparative purposes.)

D. The tutor describes a certain situation and asks the child to decide which emotion would be most appropriate for that situation. After the child correctly names the emotion, then he or she is asked to make the appropriate facial expression (which can be photographed or videotaped). For example, the tutor could tell the child the following: "It is your birthday and you have just received the exact present you always wanted. This makes you feel _____?" Then, "Can you show me with your face how you would feel?" Situations can be developed for each emotion. (TIP: Feel free to develop as many situations as you would like and individualize them for the child you are working with. Remember that the more imaginative you are at creating these situations, the more fun the child will have.)

E. The tutor asks the child to make up a story in which a certain kind of emotion will occur (anger, fear, happiness, or sadness). The child is then asked to make a facial expression to reflect that emotion. The child may make the facial expression while looking into a mirror, or while being photographed or videotaped.

Level 4: Application of Facial Cues to Daily Living

Level 4 is the most difficult level of nonverbal language training. It is the level at which the child must take the skills he or she has acquired to *discriminate, understand,* and *generate* facial expression information and *apply* these skills in social situations. Here are two formats for learning exercises in Level 4, with variations on each exercise. They can be individualized according to the needs of the child.

A. The tutor gives pictures of social situations to the child. The child is asked to explain what is happening in the picture by observing the faces of the participants. You can gather a variety of pictures from magazines, newspapers, and books. (TIP: If you find that the child has difficulty in a particular type of situation, such as play time, make sure to have a variety of pictures depicting play time.) The pictures should show all types of emotions, both genders, and adults and children should be represented.

◆ The tutor may also use *television videotapes* of social situations in the same way that *pictures* were used in exercise A. The child is asked to watch a television program (or a videotape of a particular kind of interaction) with the sound off, and then the child must judge what is happening by looking at the faces of the characters.

◆ To modify the television procedure, pause the tape while the child is watching the soundless program. Ask him or her to (1) guess what is happening at that moment and how the people are feeling and (2) predict what is going to happen next and how the people will feel. After the child makes the prediction, start the tape and show how the situation resolved itself. Discuss why the child was correct or incorrect. This exercise provides the child with practice for real-life interactions. The TV programs should include a variety of combinations of males and females, adults and children, showing many emotions.

B. The tutor explains role playing to the child. The child will be asked to imagine that he or she is in a variety of social situations and has to act in particular ways. He or she may be asked to "act like an adult who is angry" or to "behave like a happy child." One of the most important goals of role playing is to teach *when* it is appropriate to communicate incongruently and *how* to do it correctly. Children must learn that it is sometimes appropriate for them to show *in*congruence between their facial expressions and what they feel. This is especially true when politeness and manners are involved. For example, in a situation where a child does not like some food that an adult has worked hard to prepare, he or she needs to learn to squelch an expression of dislike. The exciting part of this procedure is that there's no end to the number of role-playing situations you can present. Ask the child to suggest some. The following are a few examples.

■ People are standing in line at a movie theater when someone cuts in. One person's facial expression shows anger. What has happened?

■ Children are eating lunch in school, and one of them looks disgusted. What has happened?

■ Two friends have not seen each other for years, and they see one another walking down a street. What would their facial expressions show?

■ An adult is reprimanding a child. How would they both look?

■ There is something dangerous ahead and one person has to warn the other. How would they both look?

Remediation: Some Comments

Successful remediation of one or more deficits should give a dyssemic child the nonverbal abilities necessary to better interact with others. To ensure that the child retains what he or she has learned in remediation and can manipulate this knowledge in the real world, remember to apply the three subprocesses that serve as the foundation for remediation. For example, if the child has a facial expression dyssemia, then he or she should (1) be made aware of the problem and what you are doing to improve that processing ability; (2) be encouraged to explain and practice the exercises he or she has learned to remedy the problem; and (3) be helped to apply what he or she has learned about facial expressions to the real world of his or her practical, daily interactions.

Again, children must be encouraged to remain *aware* of their potential processing difficulties, to *practice* the ways they have learned to overcome these weaknesses, and then to *apply* what they have learned to their activities with others. In our experience, applying these remediational procedures has helped children improve both their nonverbal language processing abilities and their peer relationships.

> *C*hildren must be encouraged to remain **aware** of their potential processing difficulties, to **practice** the ways they have learned to overcome these weaknesses, and then to **apply** what they have learned to their activities with others.

Fig. 8.1
Remediation can improve nonverbal language abilities and peer relationships

As we complete our thoughts concerning how best to help dyssemic children, we want to make a brief comment about the potential use of medications as part of an intervention program. While drugs of various kinds have been used in the treatment of traditional learning disabilities, they have not been broadly included in the treatment of nonverbal communication problems. However, if a child suffers from hyperactivity or an attention deficit disorder in addition to dyssemia, then use of substances such as Ritalin, Dexedrine, and Cylert (that in adults tend to energize but paradoxically in children tend to calm) may be helpful. They are generally safe when properly prescribed, and they may control hyperactivity and attention and allow a dyssemic child to focus on remediation. Please check with a knowledgeable physician regarding the possibility of a trial use of such drugs.

$\diamond$

We have only scratched the surface of nonverbal language and its implications for our social well-being. There is so much more to learn. However, we hope you are now in a better position to understand and to help those children who don't fit in. Through the identification and remediation of what we have come to call dyssemia, we can help them solve one of life's puzzles so that they, too, can share in the fullness of human interaction.

Helping Adults Fit In

Although the primary focus of this book and much of our work during the past two decades has been on dyssemic children, we have also become aware that the same problems exist throughout the life span. On the basis of our clinical experiences with, observations of, and correspondence from adults, we have come to realize that many of them also suffer from social rejection which originates from the expressive and receptive dyssemias we have identified in children and adolescents.

This is not a surprising conclusion. Without remedial efforts, many children with nonverbal communication problems simply grow into adults with the same difficulties—with one important difference: since adult relationships are more complex, dyssemias are potentially even more devastating. While nonverbal language problems in children primarily affect social and academic adjustment, in adults they can hamper interpersonal, vocational, familial, and parental functioning. Consider a letter we received from one troubled adult:

At my age, with twenty-five published articles and four advanced degrees, including a Ph.D., I face an absolutely bleak professional future. I have been out of work for most of a decade, and I have found myself so utterly oblivious to body/voice language as to be literally unable to communicate on any but the most literal levels. Hence, my inability to hold any but the most mindless of jobs—and believe me, ex-professors are rarely considered for clerk-typist spots.

I was thirty-five before a psychologist said I stood too close to people, thirty-six before another told me not to greet people with a question. My students gave me terrible reports on my teaching. . . .

No one should have to go through such hell—it was many years before I understood that everyone wasn't hostile because they seemed to be "speaking" in ways that I never imagined, and before I understood that people were put off by my apparent lack of interest because I seemed to ignore most of what they meant.

◆

The answer to the problem of social rejection in adults may be the same one we have offered for children: awareness and remediation of dyssemia. In our workshops with adults we have found that the same process of awareness, practice, and application works with adults as well. So perhaps you can apply some of the basic principles we have presented to your own adult relationships. If you do, we think you will be surprised at how helpful they can be.

REFERENCES

◇

Adler, Ronald, and Neil Towne. *Looking Out/Looking In: Interpersonal Communication.* San Francisco: Rinehart Press, 1975.

Alberg, J., C. Petry, and S. Eller. *The Social Skills Planning Guide.* Research Triangle Park, NC: Center for Research in Education, 1994.

Burgoon, Judee, and Thomas Saine. *The Unspoken Dialogue: An Introduction to Nonverbal Communication.* Boston: Houghton Mifflin, 1978.

Campbell, P., and G. Siperstein. *Improving Social Competence: A Resource for Elementary School Teachers.* Allyn & Bacon Publishing Co., 1994.

Cartledge, G., and J. F. Milburn, eds. *Teaching Social Skills to Children: Innovative Approaches.* New York: Pergamon Press, 1986.

Dowd, T., and J. Tierney. *Teaching Social Skills to Youth: A Curriculum for Child-Care Providers.* Boys Town Press, 1997.

Elias, M. J., and S. E. Tobias. *Social Problem Solving: Interventions in the Schools.* Guilford Press, 1996.

Forrester, M. A. *The Development of Young Children's Social Cognitive Skills.* Hove: L. Erlbaum, 1992.

Hall, Edward. *The Hidden Dimension.* New York: Doubleday, 1966.

Hickson, Mark, and Don Stacks. *Nonverbal Communication: Studies and Applications.* Dubuque, IA: Wm. C. Brown, 1967.

Hollin, C. R., and P. Trower, eds. *Handbook of Social Skills Training.* Oxford, NY: Pergamon, 1986.

Johnson, Doris, and Helmer Myklebust. *Learning Disabilities: Educational Principles and Practices.* New York: Gruen & Stratton, 1967.

Jourard, Sidney. "An exploratory study of body accessibility." *British Journal of Social and Clinical Psychology* 5 (1966): 221–231.

Jourard, Sidney, and J. E. Rubin. "Self-disclosure and touching: A study of two modes of interpersonal encounter and their inter-relation." *Journal of Humanistic Psychology* 8 (1968): 39–48.

King C. A., and D. S. Kirschenbaum. *Helping Young Children Develop Social Skills: the Social Growth Program.* Pacific Grove, CA: Brooks/Cole Publishing Co., 1992.

Knapczyk, P. R. *Teaching Social Competence: A Practical Approach for Improving Social Skills in Students at Risk.* Pacific Grove, CA: Brooks/Cole Publishing Co., 1996.

L'Abate, L. and M. A. Milan, eds. *Handbook of Social Skills Training and Research.* New York: Riley, 1985.

Malloy, John. *The New Dress for Success Handbook.* New York: Warner Books, 1988.

Mannix, D. *Social Skills Activities for Special Children.* Prentice Hall, 1993.

Mehrabian, Albert. "Communication without words." *Psychology Today* 24 (1968): 52–55.

Mehrabian, Albert. *Silent Messages.* Belmont, CA: Wadsworth, 1987

Minskoff, Esther. "Teaching approach for developing nonverbal communication skills in students with social perception deficits: Part I, The basic approach and body language cues." *Journal of Learning Disabilities* 13 (1980a): 118–124.

Minskoff, Esther. "Teaching approach for developing nonverbal communication skills in students with social perception deficits: Part II, Proxemic, vocalic, and artifactual cues." *Journal of Learning Disabilities* 13 (1980a): 203–208.

Morris, Desmond. *Manwatching.* New York: Abrams, 1977.

Nowicki, Stephen Jr., and Marshall P. Duke. "A measure of nonverbal social processing ability in children between the ages of 6 and 10 years of age." A paper presented at the American Psychological Society Meetings, Alexandria, VA, 1989.

Rourke, Byron. "Socioemotional disturbances of learning disabled children." *Journal of Consulting and Clinical Psychology* 56 (1988): 801–810.

Sapir, Edward. "The unconscious patterning of behavior in society." In E. Mandelbaum (ed.), *Selected Writings of Edward Sapir in Language, Culture, and Personality.* Berkeley, CA: University of California Press, 1949.

von Raffler-Engel, Walburga. "Developmental kinesics." In B. Hoffer, and R. St. Clair (eds.), *Developmental Kinesics: The Emerging Paradigm.* Baltimore: University Park Press, 1981.

OTHER RESOURCES

◇

For information about prepared materials useful in informal and formal assessment and remediation, write to Steve Nowicki and Marshall Duke, Department of Psychology, Emory University, Atlanta, Georgia, 30322.

While not exhaustive, the list of books, articles, agencies, and organizations below can provide guidance to those seeking help in understanding and working with dyssemic children.

Books:

Bimonthly Directory of Educational Facilities for the Learning Disabled. Learning Disabilities Association. 4156 Library Road, Pittsburgh, PA 15234. (412) 341-1515.

Casey, L. **Children, Problems, and Guidelines: A Resource Book for Schools and Parents.** East Aurora, NY: Slosson Educational Publications.

Cordoni, B. **Living with a Learning Disability (revised edition)** Carbondale, IL: Southern Illinois University Press, P.O. Box 3697, Carbondale, IL 62902-3697.

Dias, P. **Diamonds in the Rough.** East Aurora, NY: Slosson Educational Publications.

The Directory for Exceptional Children. Published biannually by Porter Sargent Publishers, Inc., 11 Beacon Street, Boston, MA 02108. (617) 523-1670.

Agencies and Organizations:

American Psychological Association
750 First Street, NE
Washington, DC 20002-4242
800-374-2721
www.apa.org

Council for Exceptional Children (CEC)
1110 North Glebe Road, Suite 300
Arlington, VA 22201-5704
888-CEC-SPED
www.cec.sped.org

Learning Disabilities Association (LDA)
4156 Library Road
Pittsburgh, PA 15234
412-341-1515
You can find information on each LDA state chapter at this website:
www.ldanatl.org

U.S. Department of Education—Office of Special Education and
Rehabilitative Services
400 Maryland Avenue SW
Washington, DC 20202-0498
800-USA-LEARN
www.ed.gov/offices/OSERS/

Other Useful Websites:

http://www.nifl.cov/nifl/ld/socialsk.html
Linkages: Linking Literacy and Learning Disabilities

http://www.humsci.auburn.edu/parent/socialskills.html
Encouraging Social Skills in Young Children: Tips Teachers Can Share
with Parents

http://www.kidsource.com/LDA-CA/teacher.html
KidSource OnLine: "The Teacher's Role in Developing Social Skills"

http://childparenting.about.com/parenting/childparenting/library/
weekly/aa030600a.html
"Teaching Children Social Skills and Conflict Resolution"

http://nldontheweb.org/
Home page for Nonverbal Learning Disabilities

http://www.nldline.com/
List of articles, books, audiotapes, and research on Nonverbal Learning
Disabilities

ACKNOWLEDGMENTS

◇

No book is purely the work of the authors, and this is no exception. We want to thank the hundreds of teachers and parents who have provided us with their insights and experiences in working with children who have trouble fitting in. We are also in debt to the many troubled children and adults who have shared their frustrations and achievements with us. This book is not only for them; it is in many ways by them.

We are also grateful to the wonderful people at Peachtree Publishers for their help and encouragement, especially Margaret Quinlin, Laurie Edwards, Emily Wright, Candy Magee, Kathy Landwehr, and Kathi Mothershed. Special thanks goes to the amazing group of children and adults who served as models for the photographs; they were so adept at nonverbal language that what might have been a formidable task was an absolute joy. Thanks to Max Arbes, Joy Ervin, Sharon Estroff, Abe Friedman, Stanford Ho, Marcus Legette, Anna Robinowitz, and Natanya Robinowitz.

Finally, we wish to thank our wives, Kaaren and Sara, and our children, Andy, Sharon, Noah, Jon, and Lee, for their own incomprehensible ways of supporting our endeavors.

Stephen Nowicki
Marshall Duke
Atlanta 1992

ABOUT THE AUTHORS

◇

Stephen Nowicki Jr. received his B.A. from Carroll College, his M.S. from Marquette University, and his Ph.D. from Purdue University. He is the author of over 300 publications and presentations, and is the coauthor (with Marshall Duke) of an abnormal psychology textbook and *Teaching Your Child the Language of Social Success*. During more than thirty years of teaching at Emory University in Atlanta, Georgia, Dr. Nowicki has served as director of Clinical Training, has received two Fulbright awards, and was named a Von Humboldt Scholar for research in Germany. In 2000 the Rush-Neuro Behavioral Center in Chicago bestowed upon him the Pearl Regier Humanitarian Award. Currently, he is the Charles Howard Candler Professor of Psychology at Emory, where he continues to be a consultant to public school programs and maintains an active clinical practice. He is a consulting editor for the *Journal of Nonverbal Behavior* and guest editor for nine other journals.

Marshall P. Duke received his B.A. in general psychology from Rutgers University and his Ph.D. in clinical psychology from Indiana University. After serving as a psychologist in the United States Army from 1968 to 1970, he joined the faculty of Emory University, where he is currently the Charles Howard Candler Professor of Personality and Psychopathology. He has also served as director of graduate education in clinical psychology and as chair of the Department of Psychology. In addition to having published some seventy scholarly articles, he is the coauthor (with Stephen Nowicki Jr.) of a textbook of abnormal psychology and

Teaching Your Child the Language of Social Success. With his wife, Sara Duke, he has edited *What Works with Children,* a collection of writings from forty professionals who have worked with youngsters for more than twenty-five years. An award-winning lecturer, Dr. Duke has spoken to professional and corporate groups throughout the United States and Europe. He has served as consultant to public schools for nearly three decades and continues to be a practicing clinical psychologist. He has also served as visiting research professor at Tel Aviv University, the University of London, and Exeter University in Great Britain.